AF323524

Criminal Justice
Recent Scholarship

Edited by
Marilyn McShane and Frank P. Williams III

A Series from LFB Scholarly

Could Quicker Executions Deter Homicides?
The Relationship Between Celerity, Capital Punishment, and Murder

Valerie L. Wright

LFB Scholarly Publishing LLC
El Paso 2011

Library of Congress Cataloging-in-Publication Data

Wright, Valerie L., 1975-
  Could quicker executions deter homicides? : the relationship between celerity, capital punishment, and murder / Valerie L. Wright.
       p. cm. -- (Criminal justice: recent scholarship)
  Includes bibliographical references and index.
  ISBN 978-1-59332-460-5 (hbk. : alk. paper)
  1. Capital punishment--United States. 2. Death row--United States.
3. Homicide--United States--Prevention. I. Title.
  HV8699.U5W74 2011
  364.660973--dc22
                                        2011004826

ISBN 978-1-59332-460-5

Printed on acid-free 250-year-life paper.

Table of Contents

List of Tables

Acknowledgments

I would like to begin by thanking Dr. Ruth Peterson for her continuous support and encouragement over the years. I am very grateful to have had the opportunity to work with her and have the benefit of her guidance. I would also like to thank Dr. Lauren Krivo and Dr. Bob Kaufman for taking time out of their busy schedules to offer statistical advice.

I am also thankful for the many colleagues that have given me great advice throughout this journey. Donald Hutcherson, Christie Batson, Wanda Suber, and Eileen Bjornstrom, thanks for all of your helpful comments pertaining to strategies for completing this study.

Finally, I would like to thank Patrice Dickerson and the National Science Foundation's Social, Behavioral, and Economics Science Alliance for providing funding for this project.

Chapter 1

Challenges Surrounding Long Waits on Death Row

The amount of time inmates sentenced to death spend waiting to be executed in the United States has nearly doubled during the past two decades. For example, in 1985 death row inmates spent an average of seventy-one months (5.9 years) on death row from the time they were sentenced to the actual execution. In 1990, 2000, 2005, and 2007 the average number of months spent on death row increased to ninety-five (7.92 years), 137 (11.42 years), 147 months (12.25 years), and 153 months (12.75 years) respectively (Bureau of Justice Statistics 2008). Currently, nearly 40 men have served at least 20 years on death row (Mann 2010). California has the longest delay between sentence and execution of any death penalty state with inmates spending an average of over seventeen years on death row. Currently California has nearly 697 people awaiting execution. Thirty of them have been on California's death row for over twenty-five years, 119 for at least twenty years, and 240 people have been on California's death row for over fifteen years (Death Penalty Information Center 2010).[1]

The death penalty is a punishment that continues to generate considerable debate. While many argue that the death penalty is wrong on moral grounds or that heinous criminals do not deserve to live, social scientists have primarily been concerned with issues that can be answered empirically. Since one of the major goals of the death penalty is to deter potential murderers, a great deal of the research is grounded in the deterrence literature and focuses on whether the death penalty is an effective tool for decreasing homicide rates (Bailey 1990; Bailey and Peterson 1994; Cloninger and Marchesini 2001; Peterson and Bailey 1991; Thomson 1997). Can the sanction of death deter killings if it is imposed many years after the offense has occurred? In this book, I examine whether there is a relationship between the length of time offenders wait for an execution and homicide rates. One of the tenets of deterrence theory is that punishments should follow immediately after a prohibited act so that law violators and observers alike will associate the crime with the punishment. Long delays in executions raise questions about whether the death penalty can deter killings, especially if lengthy appeal procedures and the shortage of willing and qualified attorneys extend the average time between sentencing and executions well beyond a decade.

Celerity refers to how swiftly events occur, and celerity of executions refers to the length of time between some decision point in the criminal justice system process (i.e., offense or sentence) and the execution. The issue of celerity in capital punishment has recently gained the attention of the U.S. Supreme Court. In *Thompson v. McNeil*, William

---

[1] As of November 2010, California has the largest death row population with 697 people.

Thompson, who spent thirty-two years on death row in Florida, claimed that his long-term imprisonment on death row, in addition to his death sentence, amounted to cruel and excessive punishment. The highest court declined to review the case. Nonetheless, three Justices wrote statements addressing the legalities of long waits on death row and expressed concern about the inappropriateness of excessive lengths of time spent on death row. Justice Stephen Breyer questioned whether the Constitution permits an execution after a delay of punishment for over thirty years, particularly because the state is largely responsible for delays. Justice John Stevens described thirty-two years on death row as "dehumanizing." He also noted that executing defendants after long delays is unacceptably cruel, and that the justification for such executions diminishes as the time between the homicide and punishment lapses. Moreover, Justice Stevens asserted that death row inmates typically spend twenty-three hours per day in a six-by-nine-foot cell experiencing the additional sanction of confinement. To invoke a death sentence after such a significant delay would constitute a "gratuitous infliction of suffering" (*Time on Death Row* 2005).

Justice Clarence Thomas disagreed with his colleagues asserting that the crime of murder for which the defendant is sentenced to death is what is cruel and unusual, not the punishment imposed by a jury or the appellate delays at the request of the defendant. He argues that "It is incongruous to arm capital defendants with an arsenal of 'constitutional' claims with which they may delay their execution, and simultaneously complain when executions are inevitably delayed" (*Time on Death Row* 2005:2).

One challenge to resolving the issue of excessive delays before executions lies in how to distinguish among delays resulting from a prisoner's abuse of the judicial system through submitting repetitive or frivolous appeals, a prisoner's legitimate right to appeals, and negligent or deliberate action by the state that delays execution. It is arguable that some portion of the time that elapses prior to execution may be the result of inactions by a state. In the *Thompson* case, the court declined to review the case with all its legal complexities, arguing that although the questions presented on appeal were sufficient to warrant review, aspects of the case provide a basis for delaying consideration until such issues have been researched and addressed by other courts (*Time on Death Row* 2005). Consequently, answers from the Supreme Court regarding the legalities of celerity of executions are still due, and research is needed to assist the highest court in reaching future decisions regarding what constitutes an excessive time spent on death row.

Can the sanction of death deter homicides if capital offenders wait extraordinary lengths of time before sentences are carried out? To address this question, I examine the merits of the general deterrence argument as it applies to the role of celerity of executions. Deterrence theory holds that the choice to commit murder can be controlled by the threat of punishment. The concept is rather straightforward: People will not commit murder if they believe they will be executed. A guiding principle of general deterrence theory is that punishments that are adequately severe, certain, publicized, and swift will have the greatest deterrent effect. From this view, it is possible to reduce homicides by convincing would-be murderers that they will be apprehended and punished quickly for future acts of lethal violence. Yet, very little research has addressed the link between celerity of executions and homicide rates. Thus, the extent to which the lengths of time offenders wait between the offense, conviction, or sentence and execution is associated with murder remains unknown.

While it has been argued that shorter times on death row may deprive inmates of appellate rights (Aarons 1998), one recent study has found that longer waits on death row decrease the deterrent impact of the death penalty (Shepherd 2004). If shorter times prior to executions are indeed related to reductions in state homicide rates, this suggests that efforts to speed up executions may be warranted. Unfortunately, the issue of celerity has been neglected and only a scant amount of empirical research exists on the topic. Shepherd's (2004) findings are in contradiction to an earlier study by Bailey (1980) who failed to find an effect for celerity on homicides. Beyond these two studies, with their contradictory findings, little is known about how the lengths of time inmates wait for executions impact homicide rates.

We also know little about whether certain groups, particularly racial groups, are similarly deterred (or not) by how quickly executions occur. According to the Bureau of Justice Statistics (2009), of the 37 individuals executed in 2008 twenty were white and seventeen were black. Given the social meaning attached to race in society (Bashi 1998; Bonilla-Silva 1999; Loveman 1999), it seems plausible that the deterrent message of executions may have a varying "reach" depending on the race of the executed offender or the race of the audience. Notably, deterrence theory does not assert that particular groups will be differently deterred by celerity of executions or the other aspects of punishment. To the contrary, deterrence theory assumes that audience members weigh the costs and rewards of criminal behavior equally (Gibbs 1975). However, given that racial groups have different experiences with crime and the criminal justice system, it seems conceivable that racial populations may be differentially impacted by executions, and as such be differentially deterred.

Evidence on the Relationship between Executions and Homicides

Because one of the major goals of the death penalty is to deter potential murderers (Bailey 1977; Bailey and Peterson 1987; Bohm 2007), a great deal of the research on the relationship between executions and homicide rates is grounded in deterrence theory and focuses on whether executions are an effective tool for decreasing homicides. To put the celerity argument in context, it is one of a few conditions that affect the deterrent value of punishments. Briefly, deterrence theory asserts that for punishments to be effective they should be severe, certain, made known to the public, and swift. The bulk of the long history of literature on the deterrent value of capital punishment focuses on severity and certainty and to a more limited extent publicity. As a whole, this body of work suggests that the death penalty does not effectively reduce the occurrence of homicides (Baldus and Cole 1975; Bailey 1977; Bailey 1978; Bailey and Peterson 1989; Bowers and Pierce 1975; Bowers and Pierce 1980; Peterson and Bailey 1991; Sellin 1967; Thomson 1997) and fails to support deterrence hypotheses (Bailey 1990 and Bailey and Peterson 1989; Bowers and Pierce 1980; Cochran et al. 1994; King 1978; Peterson and Bailey 1991; Stolzenberg and D'Alessio 2004; Thomson 1997; Bailey 1980; Bailey 1983; Bailey and Peterson 1987; Bowers 1983; Bowers and Pierce 1980; Cochran et al. 1994; Grogger 1990; Peterson and Bailey 1991).

Although the majority of studies suggest that the death penalty fails to deter, in recent years there have been a surge of articles by economists which conclude that the death penalty is indeed a deterrent for murder (e.g., Dezhbakhsh, Rubin, and Shepherd 2003; Keckler 2006; Liu 2004; Shepherd 2004). Based upon the results of these studies finding support for deterrence theory, Sunstein and Vermeule (2005) argue that society should be compelled to continue using the death penalty because it saves lives. However, critics describe the findings supporting deterrence theory as unreliable, asserting that the methodology (e.g., ignoring large amounts of missing data and including non-death penalty states in the analysis) and omission of key explanatory variables (e.g., sociodemographic factors) have yielded fragile results that undermine the conclusions the analysts have drawn (Fagan 2005; Fagan 2006; Nagin 1998; Weisberg 2005).

The research on celerity is by far the most scant and decidedly mixed. As previously noted, only two studies on celerity have been conducted and the authors draw conflicting conclusions (Bailey 1980 and Shepherd 2004). Specifically, Bailey's (1980) initial analysis failed to demonstrate that quicker executions are associated with lower homicide rates. Yet, Shepherd (2004), found that shorter delays on death row are associated with fewer white and black murder victims suggesting that executions serve to benefit all people. She also found that capital punishment deters crimes of passion and murders by intimates, murders previously deemed undeterrable.

Several reasons may account for why two studies would come to such contradictory conclusions. First, although many of the variables in their models measure similar concepts, the data sources and operationalizations are different, likely contributing to different results. For example, both Bailey and Shepherd control for state-level income, but Bailey uses the states' median income and

Shepherd controls for per capita income. Similarly, they both control for racial characteristics of the state, but Bailey uses the percent of non-whites in a state in his models and Shepherd uses both the percent African American and the percent of minorities that are non-African American. Second, Bailey controls for variables that are not considered in Shepherd's analysis. Bailey controls for percent urban and severity of prison sentences although Shepherd gives these variables no consideration in her analyses. These differences in control variables in the models may account for the contradictory findings.

Third, the time periods under investigation are different. Bailey examines waits on death row from 1956-1960 and Shepherd's study investigates the period from 1977-1999. It is possible that celerity of executions is not significantly related to homicides when Bailey's initial study was conducted. Perhaps this is no longer the case, and Shepherd's study has uncovered a change in the relationship between celerity of executions and homicides using more recent data. Finally, the analytic strategies used to investigate their hypotheses are different; Bailey's 1980 study uses Ordinary Least-Squares regression and Shepherd's more recent analysis relies on negative binomial regression models. In sum, there are different variables considered in Bailey's versus Shepherd's models and they use different methodological strategies which may account for the contradictory findings. Consequently, these two studies leave unanswered questions regarding the role of celerity in deterring killings. To date, the evidence is not strong enough to conclude that celerity of executions contributes (or fails to contribute) to deterrence. Thus, more research is needed to determine if speedier executions save lives by reducing homicides.

Problems Surrounding Long Waits in Solitary Confinement while on Death Row

Ironically, one point that is agreed upon in moral and political debates about the death penalty is that long a delay before the administration of a death sentence is a problem that should be addressed. On the one hand, psychologists and defense lawyers have argued that long delays on death row promote mental illness and constitute an additional punishment beyond the penalty of death (Haney 2004; Smith 2008). They describe a concept called "death row phenomena" to theorize about what has been described as the degrading treatment of condemned prisoners on death row. The three components of death row phenomena include the extraordinary long periods inmates wait for their punishment, the harsh "tomblike" physical environments in which inmates are held, and the mental anguish of living under a sentence of death. The cumulative effect of these components has been deemed a form of cruel and unusual punishment, and has been used by international courts to prevent the extradition of individuals who may face the death penalty in the United States if convicted for a capital offense (Yuzon 1996).

The issue of long waits on death row has also received recent media attention and the *Texas Observer* (Mann 2010) cites a growing body of research that describes solitary confinement in Texas as "torture." One study focused on an isolation unit in California's finds that two-thirds of inmates in solitary confinement talk to themselves, and nearly half suffered from "perception disorders, hallucinations, or suicidal thoughts" (Haney 2003). Another study found that about one-third of inmates in solitary confinement develop severe mental illness (Mann 2010). Furthermore, a 2006 report by the Commission on Safety and Abuse in American Prisons found that solitary confinement does more harm than good (Mann, 2010).

While legal and political scholars emphasize the importance of the temporal component, there is a lack of clear evidence and understanding regarding the psychological effects of the amount of time spent on death row (Smith 2008). The disconnect between psychology and the law relating to how prisoners respond to "death row phenomena" may prove to be problematic for an already complex legal issue. Thus far, two Supreme Court justices have called for further investigations given both the national and international implications revolving around capital offenders being confined for long periods under such conditions. However, despite efforts by lawmakers and victims' rights groups to make capital punishment a more efficient process, the waits on death row are becoming longer in most states (Bureau of Justice Statistics 2009). Of note, delays are not solely a result of appeals filed by inmates, but often a result of inefficiencies in a state's legal system (Aarons 1998). Such prolonged imprisonment on death row, without any clear resolution in sight to shorten waits for capital offenders, gives credence to the argument that the *Eighth Amendment's* prohibition of cruel and unusual punishment is being violated.

On the other hand, it has been argued that the long delays typically associated with a death sentence serve to weaken the deterrent effect that this punishment may have for murder-prone members of society (Shepherd 2004). Thus, from this view, restricting the amount of time that an offender has to overturn a death sentence may reduce waits on death row, thereby increasing the deterrent value of the death penalty, and ultimately saving lives (Shepherd 2004).

Another problem with long waits prior to executions is the costs associated with it. It has been argued that capital punishment debates too often overlook the issue of costs, although costs have a critical impact on other issues (Dieter 2007). Some of the most expensive costs surrounding the death penalty are related to the lengthy and complicated trials followed by incarceration and appeals (Wise 2002). Estimates on the cost of death sentences range anywhere from $216,000 (Cook 1993) to $2.3 million per year (Wise 2003). In general, capital cases on average are, five times longer than typical murder trials (Dieter 2007). They are also more expensive at every stage of the judicial process and typically require more pre-trial preparation, filed motions, and experts. In addition, twice as many attorneys are appointed, jurors are interviewed and asked about their views on the death penalty, and jurors are more likely to be sequestered (Dieter 2007). However, much of these efforts to pursue a capital sentence are in vain because, in most cases where prosecutors seek the death penalty, it is rarely imposed. More importantly, when it is imposed, it is rarely carried out. Thus, the typical death penalty case has all the expenses of its early stages and appeals; it is then overturned, and a life sentence is imposed. Overall, about twelve percent of people who have been sentenced to death are ever executed (United States Department of Justice, Bureau of Justice Statistics, 2006) although most will still spend at least some time in the most expensive area to house inmates—death row (Deiter 2007) .

Shortage of Attorneys Contribute to Longer Stays on Death Row

Inmates often wait for extended periods of time during the appellate process because they are without legal representation. For most inmates sentenced to death, obtaining an attorney is a challenge. Many attorneys are ineligible to accept death penalty cases, leaving many death row inmates waiting for legal representation, which can take several years (Aarons 1998). For example, California requires attorneys representing capital offenders to have had several years of experience in appellate cases including the handling of at least one homicide appeal (Aarons 1998). This type of eligibility requirement for attorneys handling death penalty appeals makes for a shortage of attorneys who are qualified to handle capital cases. If there are a growing number of capital offenders without counsel, it is likely that waits prior to executions will continue to become longer.

The inability of death row inmates in California to recruit lawyers for post-conviction challenges, or habeas corpus petitions, has caused a major bottleneck in the state's criminal justice system. Nearly half of those condemned to die in California are awaiting appointment of counsel for these challenges (Dolan 2010). Such shortages have persisted for years and the average wait for these attorneys is 10 to 12 years. Criminal defense lawyers attribute the scarcity to inadequate state funding, the emotional toll of representing a client facing execution and the likelihood that the California Supreme Court will uphold a capital conviction (Dolan 2010).

Finding a willing attorney to handle a capital case is another problem. For many attorneys the cost involved in defending a capital case is too much. UC Berkeley law professor Elisabeth Semel states "There are myriad reasons why dozens of lawyers who used to do these cases decide they can't afford it, I am talking about not going broke because you are trying to do the right thing for your client" (Dolan 2010: 1).

Although most capital punishment states guarantee the right to counsel for appeals, funding and resources to defend capital offenders is dwindling (Deiter 1995; Hines 2001). Many states are cutting funds for indigent defenses and private law firms are increasingly unwilling to accept capital cases because they are too expensive, burdensome, and politically unpopular. As a result, inmates often miss crucial filing deadlines for state and federal appeals challenging their convictions and sentences (Hines 2001). In 2000, there were over 230 inmates in California on death row without a lawyer to file appeals and/or petitions. By the end of 2000, some inmates with death sentences dating from 1996 and 1997 had yet to begin the first stage of the appeals process (Hines 2001). This problem is most troublesome in Alabama and Georgia, the only states that do not guarantee counsel to capital defendants. These inmates rely on death penalty resource centers and volunteer lawyers to represent them (Hines 2001). Unfortunately, capital punishment has become increasingly politicized and it has become unpopular to represent capital offenders. For decades politicians, from prosecutors to presidents, have embraced the death penalty as a symbol of their "get tough on crime" rhetoric. Therefore, it is not surprising that lawyers are not eager to take on capital cases in which they will likely be overworked, underpaid and face political scrutiny (Bright and Keenan 1995; Deiter 1995; Hines 2001) .

Given the finality of an execution, it seems necessary to ensure that capital defendants have adequate legal representation. However, this seems unlikely given the shortage of willing and qualified attorneys. While long waits on death row have been viewed as an additional punishment beyond death by some, and an unnecessary added expense by others, one study found that speedier executions will likely result in the execution of innocent people (Parkin 1999). Reducing waits for executions, therefore, seems unlikely without significant increases in resources for attorneys and/or additional limitations on appeals to reduce the workload of attorneys representing capital defenders.

Purpose of Study

The principle purpose of this study is to add to the body of capital punishment and deterrence literatures by evaluating the effect of celerity of capital punishment on state homicide rates. I examine whether the length of time before an execution is significantly related to reductions in state homicide rates as asserted by deterrence theory. Previous efforts have been made to shorten waits for executions; therefore, it seems useful to determine if reducing the waits will effectively reduce homicides. *The Antiterrorism and Effective Death Penalty Act of 1996* is an example of legislation designed to shorten waits on death row. Essentially, this law places limitations on appeals by reducing the amount of time an inmate has to file an appeal as well as the reasons that such an appeal can be filed. Although this legislation has been in place for over a decade, it is still unclear whether or not it has effectively reduced the workload of attorneys or shortened the length of time inmates wait on death row, which may increase the deterrent role of the death penalty.

I also build on the previous work on celerity by considering several points (e.g., offense, conviction, and sentence) in the criminal justice process which may be relevant for evaluating deterrence arguments. The two previous studies considered the waits between the offense and execution (Bailey 1980) and the sentence and execution (Bailey 1980; Shepherd, 2004). However, studies are needed to draw solid conclusions regarding the role of both offense and sentence celerity because the studies offer conflicting findings. Prior to the current study, the period of time between the conviction and the administration of the sentence has not been examined.

Another purpose of this work is to give attention to the "reach of executions" by assessing whether whites and blacks are equally deterred by how quickly capital punishments occur. Put differently, I ask; does the speed at which executions occur negatively impact both white and black homicide rates? I assert that celerity of executions may have a varying "reach" depending on the race of the audience and or the executionee. My interest is in how racial populations may respond differently to how quickly executions occur depending on the race of the executed and the audience. As noted by Gibbs (1975), deterrence operates through communication and relies on threat messages being effectively conveyed to potential offenders. Therefore, would-be-murderers would need to put themselves in the shoes of the person being executed in order to be deterred. If the "message" comes from executed persons that are of a different race, will the length of time prior to executions have the same deterrent impact?

In sum, prior research has given very little attention to celerity and has only rarely examined the deterrent effect of executions on specific populations. In this research, I test whether celerity matters for deterrence by examining the following research questions: (1) Does the degree of celerity in the execution of offenders significantly affect state homicide rates? (2) Does the speed of executions have varying affects on white and black homicide rates? (3) And, does celerity of executions have a differential impact on state and race-specific homicide rates depending upon whether blacks or whites are executed?

In accordance with deterrence theory, I hypothesize that the swifter the executions are carried out, the greater the deterrent effect on homicide rates will be. I argue that because deterrence theory is a communication theory and messages have to be successfully received and processed to be effective, celerity in the execution of whites and blacks may only serve to deter their own group's homicide rates. In addition, I test whether blacks and whites are differentially deterred by general executions. Although deterrence theory does not propose differential influences for members of different racial groups, given the history of the role of race and punishment in the United States, it may be that blacks are better deterred compared to whites because historically the harshest punishments have been administered to blacks (Tonry 1995). I draw from the racial identity and communication literatures and hypothesize that greater celerity in the execution of whites will deter both white and black homicides, but the execution of blacks will deter only black homicides.

Contributions to the Death Penalty Literature

In light of the scarcity of research on the effectiveness of celerity in punishment and the results of the existing studies that offer contradictory conclusions, the present investigation seeks to examine the role of celerity in capital punishments on homicide in the contemporary period. In this book I intend to contribute to the deterrence and death penalty debate in three fundamental ways. First, and most generally, I examine to what extent celerity is an aspect of capital punishment that is contributing to lower homicide rates in a period where steps have being taken to speed up executions. Legislation such as *The Antiterrorism and Effective Death Penalty Act of 1996* set a six month statute of limitation on death penalty appeals and additional limits on appellate reviews. After such an effort to shorten the overall length of time inmates spend on death row, it seems appropriate to study how variation in waits for executions impacts state homicide rates. Furthermore, it is worthwhile to focus on celerity because steps taken across jurisdictions to speed up executions are in part justified on the basis that execution delays undermine the deterrent effect of executions (Shepherd 2004). This work can further test the merits of this argument.

Second, this research will assess the scope of the applicability of deterrence theory by assessing the "reach" of the effect of celerity in executions on homicides with respect to different racial populations. I note here, that while deterrence theory assumes that all groups weigh the costs and rewards of their actions in the same way, and are equally subject to the threat of punishment, it is unclear whether all racial populations respond similarly to how quickly executions occur. Deterrence theory is in fact a communication theory and deterrence depends on the likelihood that would-be-offenders identify with those who are executed (Bowers and Pierce 1980; Gibbs 1975; Tittle 1980). From this view, messages are received best when they come from people who are similar to the person receiving the message. This raises questions of whether the swift execution of any offender deters generally or whether the person executed must be similar in background to would-be-killers for deterrence to occur. To date, no one has examined whether the race of the offender matters in this manner. I intend to provide a broader understanding of how celerity in executions of specific racial populations may matter for deterrence.

Third, this study will also shed light on the deterrent role of different measures of celerity. It is possible to define celerity in terms of the distances between executions and a variety of legal stages (e.g., offense, conviction, and sentence). Not all of these distances have been examined in the deterrence literature. Shepherd (2004) focused only on the length of time between sentence and execution and Bailey (1980) focused on only two forms of celerity: the length of time between the offense and the execution and the sentence and the execution. Perhaps other events in the criminal justice process such as the conviction may be important for gauging how long an individual waits before his or her execution is important for general deterrence outcomes. Determining the relative importance of specific measures of celerity should be useful information for those engaged in debates about curtailing the length of time offenders wait for executions by signaling which distance matters from a deterrence perspective. In addition, examining multiple time frames of celerity will aid in our understanding of the generality of the effect of celerity in executions.

Chapter 2

Deterrence Assumptions and Deterrence Research

Deterrence Theory Framework

Dating back to the Classical School of Criminology (Beccaria 1880; Bentham 1970; Hobbes 1950), deterrence theory asserts that people are rational actors that calculate the costs and benefits of their actions (Becker 1968; Gibbs 1975; Paternoster and Iovanni 1986; Zimring and Hawkins 1973). Therefore, criminal actions are events that occur when offenders decide that law-violating behavior provides greater net benefits than law-abiding behaviors. In the aggregate, general deterrence is the reduction of criminal offending stemming from the perceptions and fears the public associates with being punished (Becker 1968; Gibbs 1975; Tittle 1980). Four components of punishment have been the focus of deterrence theory: (1) certainty of punishment refers to the probability that a particular behavior will be detected and punished; (2) severity of punishment is the intensity of the punishment imposed for a specific behavior; (3) publicity of the punishment is necessary so that the public is aware of the consequences for committing particular acts; and (4) celerity of punishment refers to how immediate the punishment occurs following the criminal act. These four dimensions of punishment are thought to alter behaviors of potential offenders because from this view, the more certain, severe, publicized, and immediate the punishments, the more likely they are to produce deterrent effects. Therefore, according to deterrence theory, in order for legal sanctions to be effective deterrents to crime, they must be: (1) severe enough to outweigh any potential benefits of criminal activity; (2) administered with certainty so that the punishment is real in the minds of citizens and they come to believe that criminal actions will be detected and punished; (3) publicized to ensure that the public is aware of the consequences for breaking the law; and (4) administered swiftly so that offenders and audiences alike associate the consequences with particular crimes. Thus, general deterrence is a macro-level phenomenon that focuses on punishments that aim to prevent future criminal activities by instilling fear and impacting the rational-decision making process of potential wrongdoers. The goal is to convince those observing the punishment of others that "crime does not pay."

Ideally, would-be-offenders are to learn vicariously from the punishment of others (i.e. publicity) that illegal behavior will be detected and punished (i.e. certainty) as quickly as possible (i.e. celerity) and that the consequences will be unpleasant (i.e. severity). Most individuals prefer to avoid punishments and are discouraged from engaging in criminal behavior (Becker 1968; Gibbs 1975). Although specific individuals become the object of law enforcement activities and judicial sanctions, general deterrence is concerned with reducing the probability of offending in the general population.

With regard to homicides, the criminal justice system has the task of providing sanctions that increase the costs of homicides to dissuade would-be murderers to refrain from killings. Capital punishment, which involves taking the life of another who has wronged society gravely, is arguably the most severe sanction provided by the criminal justice system. It is utilized by some states to signal how costly it is to commit murder. As such, from a general deterrence theory perspective, capital punishment serves to protect the sanctity of life.

Research Testing Deterrence Theory Principles

Empirical research testing the role the death penalty plays in discouraging murder, has primarily focused on certainty, severity and publicity of executions. Unlike the other dimensions of punishment, celerity in executions has been given very little empirical attention. Based on deterrence principles, if a prolonged amount of time occurs between the offense and the consequences, it is unlikely that the deterrence message will have as strong an impact compared to when punishment are more immediate. Unfortunately, celerity a key component of deterrence theory is an aspect of punishment that has not been investigated nearly as much as the other dimensions of punishments. This is true even though all of the dimensions of punishment are expected to operate in conjunction with one another (Hollinger and Clark 1983). For example, a punishment cannot be expected to deter if it is severe but the level of certainty for receiving that punishment is low. If the public knows that the consequence for committing a particular offense is severe, but that only a small fraction of people actually experience this sanction they may not be deterred. Instead, people may conclude that crime does pay because the probability of being caught and punished is low. Similarly, even if the punishment is relatively severe for a particular crime, it cannot be expected to deter if the punishment is not administered celeritously. After the passing of extraordinary lengths of time, the public may associate delays in executions with a lack of punishment thereby decreasing the cost for killing. In essence, the cost of killing someone may be substantially reduced if the punishment for offenders is postponed for long periods. Applied to capital punishment and murder, the deterrence perspective would expect the rates for murder to vary inversely with measures of celerity in executions. Tests of deterrence theory have provided mixed support although as a whole this perspective has not faired well in empirical tests of the theory.

Comparative Studies of Severity. There is a long line of research on the deterrent effectiveness of capital punishment dating back to the 1920's when comparative analyses of the severity dimension of punishment focused on whether states with capital punishment had lower homicide rates compared to states that abolished capital punishment. In 1925, Sutherland was one of the first researchers to examine the correlation between homicide and the death penalty and his work illustrated that the homicide rate was lower in states and cities in which the death penalty was not provided for by law. For example, he compared homicide rates of northern states that had retained capital punishment with northern states that had abolished capital punishment. States that retained capital punishment had a homicide rate of 7.7 per 100,000 compared to abolitionist states that had a rate of 4.4 (Sutherland 1925). He also examined northern cities with populations of 100,000 or more and came to a similar conclusion; northern cities in states with capital punishment had a homicide rate of 11.3 compared to 3.1 in northern cities where the death penalty had been abolished. Although Sutherland (1925) used simple methods, his early comparisons led him to conclude that there is not a causal connection between the death penalty and levels of homicides and that legislation on the death penalty has not significantly impacted murder rates.

In Sutherland's early paper, he pointed out that such simple comparisons are inadequate because states differ on various characteristics, particularly with regard to their population composition. Thus, researchers began to compare neighboring states that were more similar on geographical, social, and economic characteristics. These studies failed to support the deterrence hypothesis as well, illustrating that even after comparing states that are similarly situated on demographic characteristics, states with capital punishment generally experience higher rates of homicide (Schuessler 1952; Sellin 1967). Schuessler (1952) compared murder rates between states that have capital punishment and states that never had capital punishment, as well as murder rates before and after changes in given states' death penalty status. He found that states without the death penalty have murder rates equal to or lower than that of death penalty states, and homicide rates were not correlated with the status of the death penalty, leading him to conclude that capital punishment has little, if anything, to do with the occurrence of murders.

Sellin, examined the period from 1920-1955 by comparing homicide rates between neighboring jurisdictions in which some had the death penalty and others did not (1967). Sellin also compared murder rates before and after states either abolished or reinstated the death penalty. Overall, he found that, jurisdictions exhibited similar murder and homicide rates despite differing on capital punishment. The findings of these studies led Sellin to conclude that the death penalty has no measurable deterrent effect beyond that of imprisonment. This perspective became the dominant view on the deterrent value of the death penalty through the 1960s.

Recently, Liu (2004) has given attention to the issue of severity by testing the relationship between murder rates and states' death penalty status. He argues that previous studies have found murder rates to be higher in states that administer the death penalty compared to states that do not execute because the decision of a state to abolish or retain the death penalty may be related to factors associated with the state such as the murder rate, political ideology, racial composition, wealth, urbanization, religion, and whether it is located in the South. Because previous studies do not control for these factors, Liu asserts that they may have mistakenly come to conclusions of a non-deterrent effect of capital punishment. In addition, he argues that states with the death penalty reduce the expected benefit of committing murder by being able to impose the sanction of imprisonment or execution whereas abolitionist states can only deter by the use of imprisonment. The probability of death is not a deterrent threat in these states, which will not produce the same degree of deterrence it could if both sanctions are deterring simultaneously. Liu (2004) found that the deterrent influence of other punishments is related to the status of the death penalty. More specifically, his study illustrated that states that abolish the death penalty lose the deterrent effect of the death penalty while simultaneously diminishing the ability of other sanctions to deter. From this study, he concludes that the death penalty deters crimes other than murder and that future studies need to account for endogenous factors that influence a states' decision to retain capital punishment. His study is one of a number of recent studies by economists that lend support to the deterrence hypothesis, although as a whole, the deterrence literature on severity suggests otherwise.

The Ehrlich Era and Certainty of Punishment. For many, Sellin's (1967) conclusion that the death penalty is unrelated to homicides suggested that the issue of deterrence and capital punishment had been settled; the death penalty is not a deterrent for murder. However, the deterrence issue got new life in the early 1970s with the publication of papers by economist Isaac Ehrlich who introduced time-series multivariate regression analysis to capital punishment and deterrence research. Ehrlich modeled the deterrent effect of the certainty of executions over time, which allowed him to simultaneously control for the effects of other explanatory variables that may impact homicide rates. Using this then new approach, he examined the effect of executions between 1933-1969 on murders controlling for demographic, economic and a time variable. Ehrlich tested whether the U.S. murder rate changed across time as the execution rate changed, and concluded that executions have a strong deterrent effect in reducing murders. Specifically, Ehrlich asserted that every execution of an offender saves on average seven to eight lives, a finding consistent with deterrence theory (1975).

Ehrlich's second study published in 1977, used cross-sectional data from 1940-1950 to test the relationship between states' annual executions and their murder rates. In this study, he includes variables similar to his 1975 study in addition to a dummy variable to differentiate between states with and without the death penalty, as well as a variable to control for median time spent in prison. Again, he found compelling evidence that the death penalty has a significant deterrent effect on homicide rates. These finding were, in turn, cited by politicians as proof that the death penalty is indeed an effective way to curtail murder rates (Radelet and Akers 1996). However, reanalyzes of Ehrlich's work has consistently failed to demonstrate a deterrent effect of executions. Researchers critiqued his studies for several reasons, including inadequacies in specifying his model and his use of unreliable homicide data. First, the effect of executions on homicides was only significant for some of the years under study and did not hold over the entire period under investigation. In addition, Ehrlich's findings are based on results from the analysis of subsamples. When other sample periods were investigated, the findings fail to achieve statistical significance (Bowers and Pierce 1975). Moreover, among the models that showed evidence of being correctly specified, the regression analysis consistently illustrated a positive, although non-significant, effect of executions on homicides.

Second, researchers argued that the Federal Bureau of Investigation (FBI) homicide data Ehrlich used was inadequate for the time period he examined because the FBI was in the initial stages and many law enforcement agencies were not yet reporting to the volunteer Uniform Crime Reports (UCR) system (Bowers and Pierce 1980; Lempert 1981). In the early 1930s only 400 agencies reported crime data to the FBI, but by 1975 over 8,500 agencies throughout the United States were reporting crimes to the FBI. As a result of such under-reporting, the FBI's national homicide data collected in the early decades of the UCR have been deemed unreliable. Bowers and Pierce (1975:187) cite a report by the National Commission on the Causes and Prevention of Violence emphasizing this problem:

> Many reporting agencies, especially in the nonurban areas, were slow in joining the UCR network; there were only 400 agencies reporting to the UCR in the 1930's, while today there are about 8,500. Thus,

trends of both violent and nonviolent crimes during the early years of the UCR are highly questionable as representative of national figures (1975:187).

Moreover, when FBI homicide rates were compared to Census homicide figures, they were fifteen percent lower than what Ehrlich estimated (Bowers and Pierce 1975) . Given all the concerns regarding Ehrlich's analyses, the result was a return to skepticism about the role of executions in saving lives.

Nonetheless, Ehrlich's work sparked renewed interest in assessing the effects of executions on homicide rates, and generated a large body of follow-up research. However, with few exceptions, the bulk of subsequent social science research, failed to demonstrate a deterrent effect for capital punishment (Bailey 1980; Bailey 1983; Bailey and Peterson 1987; Bowers 1983; Bowers and Pierce 1980; Cochran, Chamlin and Seth 1994; Grogger 1990; Peterson and Bailey 1991). In the wake of the return to capital punishment in the United States after a ten-year moratorium (from 1967-1977), researchers began to expand the scope of deterrence studies. For instance, researchers undertook analyses to examine the effect of the death penalty for specific types of murders that are most likely to be deterred by capital punishment. Some studies disaggregated homicides to examine murders that had the greatest possibility of receiving a death sentence. Bailey (1982) examined the relationship between certainty of execution for murder and police killings since most death penalty states have a provision that makes it a capital offense to kill a police officer in the line of duty. For the 1961-1967 period, Bailey found that rates of policing killings in death penalty states did not vary significantly from rates in states without the death penalty. From this finding, Bailey concluded that police in death penalty states are not provided with an additional measure of protection with the legal provision of capital punishment. However, his findings were regarded with caution because, during the 1960s, public and judicial skepticism towards the death penalty was increasing and the probability of an execution was extremely low. To address this limitation, Bailey and Peterson (1987), assessed the role of certainty of death sentences and the status of the death penalty on police killings from 1973-1984, a period in which the use of the death penalty was increasing. They found no evidence that capital punishment deters police killings. In 1994, Bailey and Peterson extended their previous studies by measuring certainty as the ratio of the number of executions for police killings to the number of police homicides rather than the ratio of total executions to the total number of homicides. They also included a measure for execution publicity. Again, they found no evidence that the death penalty provides additional protection against the killing of police officers.

Most recently however, evidence has emerged in the economics literature to suggest that the certainty of executions save lives (Cloninger and Marchesini 2001). Using a quasi-experimental design, Cloninger and Marchesini (2001) examined how changes in the use of the death penalty impact the homicide rate. From 1992-1995, Texas averaged seventeen executions per year. In 1996, there was a stay of executions for most of the year and Texas executed only three offenders. In the following year there was a twelvefold increase in executions with Texas capitally punishing a total of thirty-seven offenders, the first of which occurred in April. The dramatic increases in the use of capital punishment, following a period of limited use of capital punishment provided a unique opportunity to investigate the role of the incidence of executions. Cloninger and Marchesini (2001) found that as a result of the unofficial moratorium on executions during most of 1996, and the early months of 1997, Texas experienced an additional ninety homicides (Cloninger and Marchesini 2001). However, their findings also suggest that increases in executions may also have a diminishing effect. The deterrent effect apparently has a short memory and overtime, the effect wanes.

Dezhbakhsh, Rubin and Shepherd (2003) used county level data to investigate the role of certainty of executions on homicides. They argue that their use of disaggregated county level data provides a more detailed investigation than prior studies and allows the effects of demographic, economic and jurisdiction differences to be better captured. Controlling for two measures of certainty, the probability of an execution and the probability of a death sentence, they examined panel data for 3,054 counties from 1977-1997 to test their deterrence hypotheses. Their results indicate that each execution deters between eight and twenty-eight murders. Fagan (2006), however, cast doubt on the findings of this study because of the variables that were selected to be in the models. He argued that the instrumental variables in the model (i.e. prison admissions, Republican voters, and police payrolls) are all correlated with executions, as well as homicides, the dependent variable. In quasi-experimental designs this should not be the case because this type of model specification error biases the size of the regression coefficients and the standard errors (Fagan 2006). While these recent findings lend support to the deterrence hypothesis regarding certainty in executions, as a whole, the vast majority of the research, both prior to and after Ehrlich's famous works on certainty of executions, does not support deterrence arguments.

Research on the Role of Publicity. The research on publicity generally examines whether or not the amount of newspaper and/or television coverage of executions impacts homicide rates for some period of time after the execution publicity (Bailey 1990; Bailey and Peterson 1989; King 1978; Phillips 1980; Stack 1990). The bulk of the findings on the effects of publicity have not provided support for deterrence theory. While a few researchers (Phillips 1983; Stack 1987) demonstrate a decline in the average number of homicides for a particular period of time following publicized executions, most studies find little support for the deterrence argument (Bailey 1990; Bailey and Peterson 1989; Peterson and Bailey 1991; Stolzenberg and D'Alessio 2004). Still others have actually shown overall increases in homicides following execution publicity (Bowers and Pierce 1980; Cochran et al. 1994; King 1978; Thomson 1997).

Phillips (1980) questioned whether using yearly data, which was common in deterrence research, was the appropriate way to assess the deterrent effect of executions. He argued that executions may only deter for a short time. Thus, he used homicide data from England to examine the role of execution publicity on weekly homicide rates and found that homicides decreased temporarily by an average of thirty-six percent during the two week period immediately following the week of a publicized execution. However, in the third, fourth, and fifth weeks after the execution, the homicide rate increased, essentially negating the initial decline in killings. Although executions may produce a short-term reduction in homicides, Phillip's study provides little support for the long-term effectiveness of capital punishment as expected by the deterrence thesis.

Stack (1987) provides support for the publicity and general deterrence arguments in his study of executions stories during the period from 1950-1980 using monthly execution data. Stack distinguished between degrees of execution publicity and posited that months with highly publicized executions should have lower homicide rates than months with fewer publicized executions. Controlling for the unemployment rate and the percentage of the population in the homicide-prone age group of sixteen through thirty-four, Stack found that highly publicized newspaper stories on executions are associated with thirty fewer homicides in the same month the execution is publicized. However, Stack notes that relative to the other independent variables in the model, the relationship between less publicized executions and homicides is weak.

Bailey and Peterson (1989) extended Stack's (1987) study by using more recent execution data for a longer time frame (1940-1986). This allowed them to examine a period of time with increasing rather than decreasing execution rates while correcting for coding and measurement errors found in the Stack study. Bailey and Peterson also included omitted sociodemographic and deterrence variables. They examined rates of monthly homicides for periods leading up to, and periods following, highly publicized executions. Their analysis indicated that execution publicity is not associated with general homicide rates.

In a later analysis, Peterson and Bailey (1991) used unpublished FBI data to examine the relationship between execution publicity and felony murder, a death eligible killing. They conducted a time-series analyses to examine the effect of the amount and type of television coverage of executions on felony murder rates. Their results failed to show consistent evidence that executions and the television coverage devoted to executions are significantly related to rates of most types of felony murders. In a more recent study, Stolzenberg and D'Alessio (2004) examine the effect of newspaper publicity in Houston, using data from 1990-1994, and controlling for the possible reciprocal effects between execution risks and murders. They too found that newspaper coverage has no discernible effect on executions in Houston.

Overall, the aforementioned studies have failed to consistently show that increased publicity is associated with lower homicide rates. Unlike the previous studies that hypothesize a deterrent effect of execution publicity, Bowers and Pierce (1980) offer an alternative hypothesis to deterrence which they refer to as the "brutalization thesis." They propose that executions increase rather than decrease homicides. From this view, executions devalue human life and legitimize lethal violence demonstrating that it is appropriate to kill individuals who have wronged us (Bowers and Pierce, 1980). Furthermore, they argue that potential murderers may actually identify with the executioner rather than with the executed. With the state serving as a model, some people may be released from their inhibitions against the use of violence when settling conflicts. In their study using monthly New York data on homicides and executions from 1907-1963, Bowers and Pierce (1980) examine how the number of homicides in a given month is affected by the occurrence of executions throughout the previous year. Their findings suggest that for every execution in a month, two homicides are committed the following month. Like most of the other studies on execution publicity, Bowers and Pierce (1980) also conclude that executions do not serve to deter murders, but rather, executions are merely acts of "lethal vengeance" that encourage homicides.

Celerity in Executions and Deterrence. Although it is considered an equally important aspect of punishment, only two studies have focused on celerity as it relates to the effectiveness of the death penalty for deterring homicides. On the one hand, Bailey (1980) found that swifter executions are associated with higher homicide rates, a finding that is inconsistent with deterrence theory. On the other hand, in a more recent study, in line with deterrence theory, Shepherd (2004) found that delays in executions are associated with higher homicide rates. In brief, the two studies reach conflicting conclusions leaving us to wonder whether or not, and under what circumstances, swifter executions play a role in promoting deterrence.

In his 1980 study, Bailey argued that previous studies of the deterrent effect of the death penalty may be flawed because of ignoring the celerity aspect of punishment. Thus, previous findings on severity, certainty, and publicity may be biased because an important variable has been omitted according to the traditional deterrence thesis. He examines the deterrence hypothesis of a significant inverse relationship between state homicide rates and the: (1) celerity of the death penalty; (2) certainty of execution for homicide; (3) certainty of imprisonment for homicide; and (4) the severity of imprisonment for homicide for states with capital punishment. By testing the celerity hypothesis, Bailey offers new insight into the role the quickness of executions may play in deterring homicide, and provides a model for examining how excluding this variable may have biased previous findings.

Bailey hypothesized a positive relationship between delays in execution and state homicide rates such that as the length of time awaiting an execution increased, homicide rates would increase. Bailey uses FBI figures for murder and non-negligent manslaughter as a proxy for capital homicide rates per 100,000 in 1960 and 1960-1961, as well as unpublished data from the National Prisoners Statistic Branch of the Bureau of the Census to measure celerity as the median time in months between the death sentence and executions from the time period of 1956-1960. He measures certainty of executions as the average number of executions over a three year period divided by the number of homicides in a given year which allows for the comparison of the levels of homicide during the year under consideration as well as neighboring years. His measure of certainty of imprisonment is operationalized as the number of convicted murderers divided by the number of reported murders, and the severity of imprisonment variable is operationalized as the median length of prison sentences for murderers released in 1960. To control for other factors associated with homicide, he includes four socio demographic variables: percent of nonwhites in the population, urban population, percentage of the population aged twenty through thirty years, and median family income.

Contrary to deterrence theory, he found no evidence that delays in executions are positively related to homicide rates. In fact, the length of time between sentencing and executions for murder was consistently found to be negatively associated with state homicide rates in Bailey's 1980 study. His findings hold when the execution rate is lagged and when a three-year execution rate is used. Furthermore, although his results indicate that certainty and severity of imprisonment are negatively associated with homicides, these relationships are statistically insignificant. Finally, Bailey notes that there is no evidence to suggest that previous findings of a non-deterrent effect of the death penalty are flawed for failing to consider celerity in their models. In fact, his findings illustrate that homicide rates are better predicted by socio demographic variables such as median income, non-white population, and proportion urban than imprisonment, and they are not impacted by executions. Overall, Bailey finds no support for the deterrence argument related to celerity or certainty of the death penalty. However, he does suggest that perhaps other measures of celerity (i.e., conviction to execution) should be considered and that future studies should examine various time intervals between stages in the criminal justice process and executions.

The issue of celerity in the administration of the death penalty was ignored for over twenty years following Bailey's initial analysis until Shepherd tackled the issue again by examining the effect of executions waits on homicide as well as the deterrent effect of *The Anti-Terrorism and Effective Death Penalty Act of 1996.* This legislation put stricter limitations on convicted murderers' ability to challenge their death sentence in and effort to shorten death row waits. Shepherd (2004) argued that criminals prefer longer waits rather than shorter waits on death row as suggested by the numerous appeals and request for stays.Therefore, she hypothesized that the execution of prisoners who had a short time on death row should have a greater deterrent effect than those executions where a prisoner waited on death row for an extended period of time. In addition, she examined the deterrent effect of *The Anti-Terrorism and Effective Death Penalty Act of 1996* by assessing the probability of homicides before and after this legislation. Shepherd's study came at a time when celerity of capital punishment seemed important to legislators making death penalty policy decisions. Some opponents of capital punishment fear that innocent lives will be taken by the implementation of speedier executions, yet Shepherd argues that speedier executions may increase the deterrent effect of the death penalty, while delays in executions undermine the deterrent effect of the death penalty.

Shepherd (2004) uses Ordinary Least-Squares regression to test the effect of the length of a death row wait on the deterrence of six types of monthly murder rates: (1) the overall murder rate; (2) the rates of murder committed by intimates (i.e. spouses, common-law spouses, parents children, siblings, in-laws, and other family members); (3) the rate of murder committed by strangers; (4) the crime-of-passion murder rate (i.e. lovers triangles, murder by babysitters, drug and alcohol induced brawls, arguments over money, and abortion-murders); (5) the rates of murder of whites; and (6) the rates of murder of blacks. Shepherd examines monthly murder rates because in her view criminals form perceptions of punishment more often than once a year and base these perceptions on recent events. She also contends that the number of executions per death row inmate over the past few months is a reasonable approximation of how many people on death row are eventually executed.

Shepherd (2004) considers seven measures of celerity that represent a potential criminal's perception of how long they will wait on death row if they are executed. She uses a ratio which includes the expected delay from sentence to execution measured as the number of days the most recent executionee spent on death row, divided by the probability of an execution which she defines as a twelve-month moving average of the number of executions per death row inmate. She uses variations of this celerity measure by weighting particular months and using moving 12-month averages for both the numerators and denominator. By doing so Shepherd assumes that prisoners update their expected wait on death row with each execution and captures potential criminals' perceived risks of executions once a month instead of once a year.

In addition Shepherd includes state-level economic data from the United States Bureau of Economic Analysis from 1977-1999 and the Bureau of Labor Statistics to controls for the per capita monthly income in the state and the monthly unemployment rate for states. These economic variables serve as proxies for the labor market prospects of potential criminals, overall labor market conditions, and the availability of legitimate jobs for potential criminals. Her demographic variables are at the annual level because the percent in the population aged ten to twenty-nine years, percent male, percent minority (other than African American) and the percentage of African Americans vary little from year to year in states and vary even less from month to month.

Shepherd (2004) found that longer waits on death row before executions are associated with higher murder rates. More specifically, her results indicate that, on average, one less murder is committed for every 2.75-year reduction in the expected death row wait. Furthermore, she finds that executions serve to reduce murders for both whites and blacks and for intimates and crimes of passions. Interestingly, stranger murders and murders committed during a felony are the least impacted by this dimension of punishment. This is ironic because these are the kinds of killings that are more likely to be subject to the death penalty in the United States. Additionally, Shepherd found that the probability of executions in the months after the enactment of *The Anti-Terrorism and Effective Death Penalty Act of 1996* increased. Moreover, the coefficient for the execution rate on the post-law was larger than the pre-law coefficient suggesting that shorter death row waits increase deterrence. From these results, Shepherd concludes that lengthy waits for the administration of a death sentence diminish the deterrent value of capital punishment, and thus, future efforts aimed at curtailing long waits on death row should further increase the death penalty's deterrent value.

Limitations of Previous Research on Celerity

The above research fails to provide a consistent pattern regarding the effect of celerity in executions on homicides. While Bailey's (1980) findings fail to support the hypothesis, Shepherd's (2004) more recent study concludes that quicker executions have a deterrent effect. These conflicting findings, raise questions about the true role celerity has in producing deterrence. The current study will attempt to shed further light on the relationship between this dimension of punishment and deterrence.

To date, research on celerity has only examined the lags of time between offense to execution (Bailey, 1980) and sentence to execution (Bailey, 1980; Shepherd, 2004). However, it is plausible that researchers have not truly identified the point during the criminal justice process that is meaningful for studies on celerity. For example, the conviction may be an optimal point in the criminal justice proceedings that the public may associate with the offense. Unlike, an arrest, a conviction for murder, almost always is followed by a formal sanction, and therefore, the time between conviction and execution may have an effect on the decision making of potential offenders. In addition, the formal sentence to death, although it often comes months or even years after an initial arrest, may be a point in the judicial process that more members of the public are likely to remember and associate with the murder. In an effort to more thoroughly test the role of celerity, I will explore the relative importance of time lags between the various stages of the justice process: offense, conviction, and sentence relative to the execution.

Finally, the research on the deterrent value of the death penalty has only rarely examined whether the dimensions of punishment have similar deterrent effects on specific types of homicides. Peterson and Bailey (1991) have examined felony homicides and police killings (Bailey and Peterson, 1994). However, little research has been done to examine the deterrent effect on specific racial populations. To date, the only study to assess whether celerity in executions impact both black and white homicide rates is Shepherd (2004). She found that shorter stays on death row are related to lower rates of homicide for blacks and whites. However, we do not know how the race of the person being executed influences homicides for different racial groups. Do all executions deliver the same deterrence message, or does it matter if deterrence messages come from individuals that are similar in race? Although Shepherd's recent work suggests that executions deter the homicides of both blacks and whites, neither Bailey's nor Shepherd's work on celerity considered how race may alter the effectiveness of celerity in executions for producing deterrence from killings. In other words, neither study assessed if the race of the offender mattered. Yet, deterrence theory is fundamentally a communication process that relies on potential offenders receiving threat messages regarding what the consequences could be if they commit similar offenses. Race may be an important characteristic for how responsive audiences are to such a threat message.

Why Race May Matter For Deterrence

Early work by Tittle (1975) observed the need for deterrence theory and researchers to explain variations in the frequency of violations among demographic categories of the population. Observing others being sanctioned may produce deterrence depending on the characteristics of the population being deterred (DeLamater 1968). It seems reasonable that people with different social classes, ages, sexes, and races may respond differently to observations of punishments. To date, only Shepherd's work demonstrates that swifter executions serve to decrease the homicide rates of both blacks and whites (2004). At the same time, previous research has shown that blacks and whites vary in their perceptions of the perceived probability of apprehension (Waldo and Chiricos 1972) and severity of punishment for law violations (Wood and May 2003). Such different perceptions could signal variation in the consequences of punishment practices for different racial groups including in terms of deterrence from crime. Yet, we only have one study that provides evidence on celerity in executions and deterrence for blacks and whites. In the following paragraphs, I offer reasons why race may matter for deterrence messages. I argue that racial identity, and different perceptions of and experiences with, the criminal justice system, may affect how the deterrence message in the execution of black and white offenders may have a varying "reach."

Racial Identity and Deterrence. Racial identity is a social construct that refers to a sense of collective identity based on one's perception that he or she shares a common heritage and fate with a particular racial group (Helms 1993). In addition, racial identity describes our inclination to categorize others, often based on skin color. It reflects how we see ourselves, how we see those whom we share a racial classification with, and how we perceive individuals outside our own racial category (Helms 1993). People tend to relate on a more personal level and are more likely to feel as though they have more in common with people who are similar in race to them (Newcomb 1961). Most often racial groups identify with others that share similar traditions, values, and beliefs allowing all groups to make sense of the world around them and how their particular group is situated in that world (Chavez and DiBrito 1999).

Bowers and Pierce (1980) argue that potential offenders must identify with executionees in order for deterrence to occur. They must be able to place themselves in the shoes of the person being executed and envision themselves experiencing the same consequence if they were to commit the same act. This raises questions about whether racial identity matters for deterrence.

Populations with considerable political and economic power have a history of defining their own racial/ethnic group as being superior to others (Bashi 2000). Whites, the largest racial group in the United States, have historically used race as a characteristic by which they make decisions about whom it is appropriate to attend school with (Smith 1981), socialize, and marry (Thernstrom and Thernstrom 2002). In addition, whites have made considerable efforts to distinguish themselves from blacks by opposing the Civil Right's Movement (Morris 1999; Thernstrom and Thernstrom 2002), through residential integration (Massey 1990; Thernstrom 2006; Wilson 1987), and even establishing the "one drop rule" which holds that a person with any trace of African ancestry is considered black (Thernstrom 2000).

Given the social importance placed on racial identity in society, and the history of discrimination and racism, strong feelings toward those of the same and differing races have developed and racial groups tend to socialize and develop networks amongst themselves (Helms 1993; Newcomb 1961). This racialized socializing may cause deterrence messages to be taken more seriously if the persons being executed are similar in race to the audience. For example, the execution of a white offender may signal to the white and black population that even law violators who are a part of this "superior" race are eligible for the death penalty. However, a different message may be signaled to blacks and whites observing the execution of another black. Given the long tradition of blacks receiving more severe punishments compared to whites (Tonry 1995), the execution of blacks may serve to deter observing blacks. However, for observing whites, the executions of blacks may signal that the state is doing business as normal, and imposing a death appropriately on people unlike themselves. Thus, black executions may fail to produce deterrence for white homicides.

Racial Identity and Communication. Previous research in the communication literature also suggests that racial populations tend to respond "best" when messages are delivered from members of the same race (Pitts, Whalen, O'Keefe and Murray 1989). Central to this racially based approach to communication is the idea that racial groups may be more likely to see themselves in the shoes of the messenger if they appear to share an ethnic background (Bashi 1998; Bonilla-Silva 1999). Whether this tendency to "identify" with those who are racially similar is the result of limited exposure to members of other races, fear, or mere ignorance, this relationship is so well understood that companies use race in advertising to better market their products (Liss 1981; Pitts et al. 1989; Whittler 1991; Whittler and Spira 2002).

Studies assessing the use of racial cues in product advertising suggest that groups respond differently based on the race of the person advertising the message (Pitts et al. 1989; Whittler and Spira 2002). In a study assessing whether blacks and whites respond differently to culturally targeted commercials, Pitts and his colleagues (1989) found that blacks have a more positive perception of commercials featuring black actors than do comparable whites. In another study, Whittler and Spira (2002), examined the influence of actors' race on black and white viewers' attitudes and purchase intentions and found that blacks evaluate products and advertisements that use black models more favorably than those advertised by white actors (2002). Similarly, whites responded better to products advertised by white actors and perceive themselves as less similar to, and are less likely to identify with, black actors (Whittler and Spira 2002). Because the studies offered identical products and only manipulated the race of the actor, the findings suggest that irrespective of the content of the message, race plays a part in how audiences interpret the message as being intended for them.

The link between communicating messages and racial identity is also evident in the racial preferences of children. Studies indicate that children's preferences for playmates (McCandless and Hoyt 1961), dolls (Hraba and Grant 1970), and pictures (Liss, Newman and Sherman 1979) follow same-race patterns. In addition, when black and white children are provided with equal access to predominately black and white television programming, they are significantly more likely to choose television shows that have a cast that is predominantly the same race as them (Liss 1981). These patterns of racial preferences illustrate that same-race individuals may be able to better capture the attention of others in their racial group.

Somehow, racial similarity elicits a more desirable response because the messages conveyed are coming from people with whom like individuals can identify. This implies that the race of the "model" can indeed impact the effectiveness of conveying a message. If messages come from sources that are dissimilar in race, to some degree, the impact of the message may be diminished. Racial identity may also influence deterrence. It seems plausible that racial groups may be more deterred by celerity in the executions of those who look like they are similar in race to them. The swiftness in executions of different racial groups may not deter racially conscious audiences from committing homicides, if they view members of racially dissimilar groups as being so different that they cannot place themselves in that person's shoes.

Racial Differences in Perceptions of the Criminal Justice System. Survey data suggests that blacks and whites have very different perceptions of the criminal justice system (Bobo and Johnson 2004; Brunson 2007; Henderson, Cullen, Cao, Browning, and Kopache 1997). Varying perceptions of the criminal justice system may influence whites and blacks to be differentially deterred by celerity in executions of members of differing races. Many blacks believe that the criminal justice system is harsher toward blacks relative to other racial and ethnic populations (Bobo and Johnson 2004; Brunson 2007) . On the other hand, whites generally believe that the system is racially neutral and reflects the ideal of equal treatment under the law (Henderson et al. 1997). Surveys and polls consistently indicate that a larger proportion of blacks than whites have unfavorable opinions about various components of the justice system including the police (Maguire and Pastore 2002; Wortley, Hagan, and Macmillan 1997), courts (Roberts and Stalans 2000), and lawyers (Henderson et al. 1997; Roberts and Stalans, 2000).

In a recent study, Maguire and Pastore (2002) found that, compared to whites, blacks are more likely to fear being stopped and arrested by the police when they are innocent (42% versus 16%), and to feel that the courts are too harsh on criminals (14% versus 6%). Studies have also revealed large racial and ethnic group differences in support for the death penalty such that minorities, particularly blacks, are less likely to support the death penalty compared to whites (Bobo and Johnson 2004) . In their study using a nationally representative sample assessing how black and white Americans hold different views about the use of capital punishment, Bobo and Johnson (2004) found that just over eighty percent of whites compared to only fifty percent of blacks favor the death penalty for people convicted of murder. This is not surprising given the racial differences in support for conservative political parties (Unnever and Cullin 2007), for the police (Halim and Stiles 2001; Sunshine and Taylor 2003), and perceptions regarding the criminal justice system (Young 1991; Hagan and Albonetti 1983; Henderson et al. 1997). In each case, blacks are less inclined to believe that they are treated fairly by the institution. The fact that fewer blacks support the use of the death penalty may be partially conditioned by the fact that many in this population view it to be a coercive tool to further perpetuate inequities against blacks.

As a result, of groups identifying more strongly with members of their own race, when a white is executed, it may signal to both the black and white populations that the criminal justice system is particularly aggressive in their efforts to combat homicides. Since blacks are more likely to view themselves and other blacks as being treated more harshly than whites, at the very least, blacks would expect to get the same or worse punishment as a white for committing a capital offense. Consequently, this perception of inequity in the treatment of blacks may cause blacks to be more responsive to swift executions, relative to other populations because, historically, the system in place to control criminal behavior is one that is perceived as racially biased.

Moreover, blacks are more likely than other racial populations to have encounters with the criminal justice system (Johns 1992; Mann 1993). This increased frequency in contact with the criminal justice system may serve as a reminder to blacks that their behavior is being more closely scrutinized relative to whites. As such, blacks may be more likely to refrain from committing crimes than whites who may not be deterred from offending as a result of their less frequent contact with the criminal justice system. This seems particularly likely because the increased contact with the criminal justice system may convince blacks that their racial group is more likely to be punished following the commission of a crime.

It is so common for sanctions to be used as tools of social control against members of subordinate groups that one can easily identify which groups are subordinate within the social structure by noting which groups are overrepresented in that society's prisons (Sidanius, Mitchell, Haley, and Navarrete 2006). Perception of inequity may cause the black population to be deterred by celerity in the execution of whites toward whom they view the system as being more lenient. Whites, however, who are more inclined to support the death penalty, may associate a "swifter" execution of blacks as the criminal justice system performing one of its normative functions. Thus, black executions, regardless of how quickly they are carried out, may do little to dissuade would-be white murderers who may view the execution as merely a means by which the criminal justice system deals with the "criminalblackman" (Russell 1998).

In sum, it is possible that race matters for deterrence for several reasons. First, groups tend to form racial alliances, and are more likely to identify with others that are similar in race to their group (Helms 1993). As a result, threat messages in the form of executions may only be effective if they come from members of the same race. Second, general deterrence is a communication theory that relies on threat messages being received. As such, groups must be able to place themselves in the shoes of the executed. If these execution messages are from a racial group that is different, the message may not have the desired impact. Finally, blacks and whites have different perceptions of the criminal justice system and their treatment by it. Blacks are more likely to believe that they are mistreated by the justice system while whites generally view the justice system as racially impartial (Bobo and Johnson 2004; Brunson 2007) . In addition, blacks have more frequent contact with the criminal justice system and this may serve to remind blacks that their behaviors are being monitored more closely than those of whites. As a result, they may be deterred from committing murders for which whites may not be deterred. Overall, there are reasons to suspect that race may matter for deterrence and this work will investigate whether this suspicion is warranted.

The conceptual arguments presented above have not been explored and it is unclear whether celerity in executions has a varying reach. In the race-specific analyses, I will assess: (1) whether executions, regardless of the race of the executionee, have a differential impact on race-specific homicide rates; and (2) whether race-specific homicide rates are differentially influenced by the race of the person being executed. This will broaden the scope of research on deterrence and address the issue of whether two important and distinct United States populations are equally deterred by general executions, and whether both groups produce deterrence equally on general and race-specific homicide rates.

Research Hypotheses

Based upon theoretical inferences and previous work, I test several hypotheses to examine the relationship between celerity in executions and homicide rates. In general, I expect states that execute more swiftly to have lower homicide rates than states that take a longer time to execute.

Research on celerity has only examined the lags of time between offense to execution (Bailey 1980) and sentence to execution (Bailey 1980; Shepherd 2004). The time between convictions and executions has not been examined as an aspect of celerity that may affect homicides. However, it is plausible that researchers have not truly identified the point of punishment that is meaningful for studies of celerity. The focus of the deterrence perspective is on the time between the commission of the offense and the punishment. It suggests that punishments are most effective when they are administered as soon as possible after the commission of an offense. Therefore, the gap elapsed between the offense and the execution may need to be considered when operationalizing the length of time between the offense and the consequence for committing the offense. Similarly, the conviction may be a point in the criminal justice proceedings that may signal the initiation of punishment since arrests do not always lead to a formal sanction. Unlike committing an offense, a conviction for murder, almost always is followed by a formal sanction, and therefore, the time between conviction and execution may affect the decision making of potential offenders. In addition, since the formal sentence to death may be the most definitive stage leading to the execution it may be useful to investigate the role the time from sentence to execution bears on deterring homicides. Thus, in an effort to more thoroughly test the role of celerity, I will explore the relative importance of time lags between the various stages of the justice process: offense, conviction, and sentence relative to the execution. I offer the following hypotheses:

H1: Shorter offense, conviction, and sentence gaps prior to executions will be negatively associated with overall homicide rates.

The research on the deterrent value of the death penalty has only rarely examined whether the dimensions of punishment have similar deterrent effects on specific populations (i.e., group-specific homicides). Shepherd (2004) found that quicker executions are significantly related to reductions in the black and white homicide rates. However, one study does not offer enough empirical evidence to make broad generalizations and more studies are needed to support this claim. It is possible that blacks and whites are differentially deterred by how quickly capital offenders are executed. Thus, I examine whether the role of celerity of executions in black versus white homicides is consistent with the classical arguments that people weigh the costs and rewards of crimes and associate punishments in similar manners, or whether the impact of the swiftness in executions varies by race. To address this question, I test the following hypothesis:

H2: Shorter waits prior to in executions will have a negative effect on both white and black homicide rates.

Finally, the race of the person being executed could also impact the deterrence message being sent. We currently do not know whether it matters if deterrence messages come from individuals who are similar in race to the targeted audience. Previous work on celerity does not consider how the race of the executionee may alter the effectiveness of celerity in executions for producing deterrence. I note here again that deterrence theory is race-neutral; it does not suggest that racial similarity between the punished and the observers of punishment is a prerequisite for deterrence to occur. However, since deterrence theory is a communication theory that relies on potential offenders receiving threat messages regarding what the consequences could be if they commit a similar offense, race may be an important characteristic for how responsive audiences are to such messages. Thus, I offer the following hypotheses:

> *H3: Shorter waits before white executions will have a significant negative effect on white homicide rates.*

> *H4: Shorter waits before black executions will have a significant negative effect on black homicide rates.*

> *H5: Increased celerity in the execution of whites will have a significant negative effect on black homicide rates.*

> *H6: Increased celerity in the execution of blacks will not be significantly related to white homicide rates.*

Chapter 3

Description of the Data Sources and Analytic Strategy

In the current analysis, I use state-year level data to better understand the role of celerity in state homicide rates controlling for percent metropolitan, levels of disadvantage, percent young males, Southern region, and time periods (1991-1995, 1996-2000, and 2001-2004). I also control for certainty in executions and employ dummy variables to account for state-year groups without executions and state-year groups without any individuals waiting on death row.

Data Sources

To examine whether swifter executions effectively reduce the occurrence of homicides, including homicides for different racial groups, multiple data sources are employed. Data on homicide offenders comes from the Federal Bureau of Investigation's (FBI) Supplementary Homicide Reports for the years 1995, 2000, and 2004. These data are part of the Uniform Crime Reporting (UCR) program and captures information on each homicide incident reported by law enforcement agencies. Importantly, supplemental homicide incident data are submitted monthly with details on the state, information on the offenders and victims that were involved, (including race) which allows for race-specific analyses.

Capital punishment data are from *Capital Punishment in the United States, 1973-2004* from the United States Department of Justice, Bureau of Justice Statistics. This series provides annual data on prisoners under a death sentence and are particularly suited for the current analysis because it includes demographic data on prisoners such as their race, as well as the dates of their offenses, convictions, and executions which are needed to construct the celerity measures.

To avoid spurious results while assessing the relationship between the independent variables and homicides, the models include controls for several sociodemographic variables that have been found to affect homicides. The sociodemographic control measures were constructed using data from the U.S. Bureau of the Census, Population and Housing Summary Tape File 3 (STF3) for 1999 and Summary File (SF3) for 2000. The variables for the period 1991-1995 use 1990 Census data, the variables for the period 2001-2004 use 2000 Census data, and the variables for the period 1996-2000 use the average of the 1990 and 2000 Census data with the exception of the poverty measure. Data on poverty come from 1989 and 1999 and data for the period 1996-2000 uses the average of the data from 1989 and 1999. These data contain responses from questionnaires asked of a sample of people in all housing units in the United States and allow for the calculation of the disadvantage index, percent young males, and Southern region measures. Data on percent metropolitan is obtained from the *Statistical Abstract of the United States, 1997* and Statistical Abstract of the United States, 2006 which are published by the United States

Department of Commerce Economics and Statistics Administration: Bureau of the Census.

The Sample

The analysis is limited to the thirty states that provided for the death penalty from January 1, 1991 through December 31, 2004. These include Alabama, Arizona, Arkansas, California, Colorado, Connecticut, Delaware, Florida, Georgia, Idaho, Illinois, Indiana, Kansas, Kentucky, Louisiana, Maryland, Mississippi, Missouri, Montana, Nebraska, Nevada, New Hampshire, New Jersey, New Mexico, New York, North Carolina, Ohio, Oklahoma, Oregon, Pennsylvania, South Carolina, South Dakota, Tennessee, Texas, Utah, Virginia, Washington, and Wyoming.[2] The unit of analysis is state-year groups such that each case is a state during a specific period. Thus, each state has three cases corresponding to the periods 1991-1995, 1996-2000, and 2001-2004. In total, there are 111 state-year groups in the analysis.[3]

The Measures

To examine the role of celerity in deterring homicides, I conduct analyses using several theoretically based measures controlling for sociodemographic factors. Table

---

[2] Kansas did not reinstate its death penalty until April 22, 1994. New York did not reenact capital punishment until September 1, 1995 and on June 24, 2004, New York declared capital punishment unconstitutional. Connecticut, Kansas, New Hampshire, New Jersey, New York and South Dakota were all death penalty states but did not execute anyone during the years included in the current study. These states are included in the analyses.

[3] Homicides were not reported to the FBI by Kansas in 1995, Florida in 2000, or Florida in 2004. As a result of missing homicide data, there are only 111 cases.

3.1 presents the operationalizations of the dependent, independent and control variables used in the study and serves as a reference for the discussion below.

State Homicides Rates as the Outcome Variable. Homicides as defined in this analysis include murder and non-negligent manslaughter, which is the willful killing of one human being by another. Thus, the analyses exclude deaths caused by negligence, accidents, killings during terrorists' acts, and justifiable homicide.[4] General homicide is operationalized as a count of homicide offenders for each state and the respective time periods. In the following chapters, to allow for a more straightforward interpretation, I report the rates of homicides although the variable is constructed as a count. The homicide rate is calculated by dividing the number of homicides into the total state population and multiplying that product by 100,000. I specify the negative binomial regression model so that it transforms counts into a rate which is reported in the results. In addition, race-specific measures of homicide were created for the race-specific analyses. The white and black homicide counts include only homicides committed by members of the respective races.

Celerity Measures. In the current analysis, I employ three measures of celerity for all states and periods under study: (1) time from offense to execution; (2) time from conviction to execution; and (3) time from sentence to execution. The celerity measures represent the number of months elapsed between the offense, conviction, and sentence and the execution. To calculate these gaps, I sum the total of the execution year multiplied by twelve with the

---

[4] The deaths caused from the September 11, 2001 bombing are not counted as homicides by the Bureau of Justice Statistics and are thus not included in the current analysis. I report the rates of homicides although the variable is constructed as a count.

number representing the execution month (i.e. 1=January, 2=February etc…). Next, I subtract the gap year multiplied by twelve and add the sum to the number representing the gap month. Specifically, these measures were calculated using the following three equations:

1. Offense Celerity: *[(execution year*12) + execution month]-[(offense year*12)+ offense month]*
2. Conviction Celerity: *[(execution year*12) + execution month]-[(conviction year*12) + conviction month]*
3. Sentence Celerity: [*(execution year*12) + execution month]-[(sentence year*12)+ sentence month]*

An additional celerity dummy is included to control for state-year group combinations where no one was executed. To account for the fact that some death penalty states did not execute anyone in a given period, I include a celerity dummy measure coded as zero if an execution occurred in the state-year group and coded as one if there were no executions. Thus, the inclusion of this dummy variable allows for the distinction between states with and without executions during a period. To provide a comprehensive examination of celerity, I also include a measure for prisoners under a sentence of death but who were not executed during the periods of study. This measure is operationalized as the average number of months non-executed prisoners spent on death row.[5] Including this

---

[5] For those persons sentenced to death more than once, the numbers are based on the most recent sentence to death. The United States Department of Justice, Office of Justice Programs; Bureau of Justice Statistics does not calculate the average amount of time spent on death row for states with fewer than ten persons awaiting an execution. The average time spent on death row was calculated using the midpoint

measure allows for a more inclusive operationalization of celerity of executions. It includes offenders who were sentenced to death and who spent time on death row as opposed to only offenders that were executed.[6] A dummy for the average time alive on death row is also included to control for states and periods where no one was on death row.[7] The inclusion of the dummy variable allows for the zeros representing the missing data on the time on death row variable to be interpreted as no one on death row rather than less than one month spent on death row.

Certainty. To control for variation in states' likelihood of executions, I include a measure of certainty of execution. In models of total homicide, I include a general measure of certainty operationalized as the number of executions during the respective time period. Standardizing the number of executions by dividing them by the number of death sentences is not necessary because it is unlikely that potential murderers are aware of the number of death sentences (Berk 2005) that are given by the courts in the state. Therefore an execution count better captures the public's perception of certainty of executions. In the race-specific analyses, certainty is operationalized as the total

---

from the year(s) of sentence until the respective years 1995, 2000, and 2004. The states that were not calculated include: (1995) Connecticut, Montana, New Mexico, South Dakota, and Washington; (2000) Colorado, Connecticut, Montana, New Mexico, New York South Dakota, and Wyoming; (2004) Colorado, Connecticut, Illinois, Maryland, Montana, Nebraska, New Mexico, New York, South Dakota, and Wyoming.

[6] The average number of months on death row variable includes prisoners who were likely exonerated or died prior to their execution.

[7] States that did not have anyone on death row include: (1991-1995) Kansas, New Hampshire, New York, and Wyoming; (1996-2000) New Hampshire; (2001-2004) Kansas and New Hampshire

number of whites, or blacks, executed during each respective period under investigation.

Based on the evidence of prior research, and to control for spuriousness, several sociodemographic factors that have been linked to homicides are included in the analyses. Studies have shown that homicide rates are affected by the proportion of the population that is disadvantaged, young and male, and in metropolitan areas. Homicides also tend to be higher in Southern states. Consistent with prior research, I expect that variables capturing these conditions will be positively associated with homicide rates.

Disadvantage. Wilson (1996) and Sampson and Wilson (1995) emphasize that crime, including violent crime, is one of the many consequences of living in areas characterized by high levels of poverty, female-headed households, and unemployment. These structural barriers to conventional success contribute to higher levels of crime. Prior research has linked structural disadvantage to violent crime for various units of analysis (Krivo and Peterson 2000; Kublin and Weitzer 2003; Lee and Ousey 2007; Peterson and Krivo 1999; Silver 2000). Sampson and Wilson (1995) point out the negative consequences of living in disadvantaged areas characterized by high levels of poverty, female-headed households, and unemployment. Not surprisingly, the measures for poverty, female-headed households and unemployment are highly correlated. As a result, I constructed an index that combines the three indicators of structural disadvantage. These three indicators were transformed into z-scores and averaged. The result is a disadvantage index with a mean of zero and a standard deviation near one. The reliability estimate (Cronbach's alpha) for the disadvantage measure is .76. In this research, I argue that states with higher levels of disadvantage will have higher rates of homicide.

Poverty. Poverty is defined as the percent of the state population for whom poverty status is determined and whose income in 1989 or 1999 was below the poverty level. Numerous articles using various units of analysis have linked poverty to high rates of crime (Lee 2000; Shaw and McKay 1942) and homicide (Land, McCall, and Cohen 1990; Lee 2000; Sampson and Groves 1989; Krivo and Peterson 1996). Various theoretical perspectives propose that poverty is related to violent crime including macro-level strain theory. According to strain theory, crime breeds when there is a disjuncture between aspirations for economic success and the means to achieve economic success (Merton 1938). Messner and Rosenfeld (1994), argue that the "American Dream" is a cultural goal that entails a commitment to the goal of economic success. From this view the cause of crime is a form of anomie and the pursuit of the "American Dream" fosters anomie because oftentimes the quickest way to material success is rooted in crime. Thus, poverty is a form of goal blockage (Merton 1968) and the severe economic conditions experienced by the poor essentially remove traditional routes to goal achievement. When economic concerns are high, there are going to be portions of society that will compare the economic conditions of others to their own economic conditions and may perceive themselves as being deprived relative to others around them (Merton 1938). The ability to use violence and a predatory demeanor may serve to provide economically deprived groups of society with an alternative route to achieving status. In poverty stricken areas violence, including the taking of human life, is oftentimes viewed as a means to an end and violence can earn respect from one's peers and one's enemies, as can traditional means of acquiring economic success (Sampson and Wilson 1995). For example, in areas characterized by poverty, it is commonplace for trivial conflicts to be settled with aggressive responses or even acts of violence (Anderson, 1999). The ability to display a readiness to use violence and a predatory demeanor is part of an ethic of honor among many of the poor. Thus, acts of violence including homicides are essentially adaptations to extreme economic conditions (Lee 2000).

Female Headed Households. The percentage of female-headed households is also included in the disadvantage index as an indication of family disruption and represents the percentage of households in the state with a female head and minor children. Female-headed households have been one of the most common explanations of crime trends in the United States (LaFree 1999) and have been shown to be associated with higher homicide rates (Almgren, Guest, Immerahr, and Spittel 1998; Rosenfeld 1996; Sampson 1987; Sampson and Groves 1989). A key finding of Sampson's (1987) analysis was that homicides are strongly predicted by family disruption, which in turn, is the result of joblessness and poverty. This effect was found for both blacks and whites. Sampson (1987) argued that family formation and stability are largely dependent upon the ability of males to be gainfully employed. Structurally, stable two-parent families are buffers against violent crime, and areas with higher rates of female-headed households have fewer guardians to exert control over minors. Therefore, single parents are less able to monitor the social activities and associations of their children. An added factor is that unwed mothers are particularly vulnerable to poverty and are likely to reside in poor, crime-ridden areas where collective capacity to control the behavior of children is lacking (Shihadeh and Steffensmeier 1994). Particularly in these types of areas, rates of violent crime are likely to increase. Although other theoretical perspectives emphasize different dynamics of how family structure impacts crime, in general they suggest that families help to regulate crime rates by serving as the primary institution for socializing children, passing values from one generation to the next, regulating the behavior of their children, restricting their activities, and maintaining surveillance over them (LaFree 1999).

Unemployment. Unemployment is another structural factor that has been linked to rates of homicides. In this study unemployment is operationalized as the percent of the civilian population aged sixteen and over in the labor force who are not working, actively seeking work, and available to accept a job. Researchers using various samples, units of analysis, and methods have found that unemployment rates are associated with higher rates of violent crime (Almgren et al. 1998; Krohn 1976; LaFree 1999; Sampson 1987). Sampson (1987) found that violence and homicides escalate when there are extreme levels of unemployment, especially among young men. The idea that crime is a function of high levels of economic stress, oftentimes measured as rates of unemployment, has been explained by several otherwise competing theories including social disorganization (Kornhauser 1978), social strain (Cloward and Ohlin 1960; Merton 1938), violent subcultures (Wolfgang 1967), and routine activities (Cohen and Felson 1979) among others. While the specific arguments diverge enormously, most of the theories assert that economic stress undermines commitments to legitimacy and weakens social bonds (LaFree 1999).

Percent Young Males. It is widely recognized that there is a relationship between age and crime (Gartner and Parker 1990; Hirschi and Gottfredson 1983). Teens and young adults, particularly males, commit crimes more frequently than those in other age groups and are more likely to be both offenders and victims of crimes (Gartner and Parker 1990). In their cross-national analysis of the impact of age structure on homicide rates, Gartner and Parker (1990) found that increases in the proportion of young males have a positive and significant effect on homicide rates in the United States and Italy. To date, most studies on the effects of age structure on homicide report a significant positive relationship with the proportion of young people in the population. In fact, of the twenty-four studies of homicide reviewed by Marvell and Moody (1991), sixteen of them found a strong or moderate relationship between age structure and the murder rate. To control for the effect of the most crime prone portion of the population, I include young males as a control. It is operationalized as the total number of males in a state aged sixteen through thirty-four divided by the total state population. The race specific measures include young males in the respective black and white populations.

Southern Region. Research on the spatial distribution of crime has consistently shown that the South is the most violent region in the United States (Gastil 1971; Lee, Hayes, and Thomas 2008; McCall, Land and Cohen 1992; Simpson 1985; Wolfgang and Ferracuti 1967). A dummy variable for Southern region is included in the analysis to control for what previous research has deemed a unique value system in the South referred to as the "subculture of violence" that reinforces violent behavior. Macro-level studies of crime have shown that Southern region is significantly related to murders, (Blau and Blau 1982; Messner 1982; Rosenfeld 1985). Testing the subculture of violence thesis, Rosenfeld (1986) shows that South is a significant predictor of murder and assaults. Thus, since fifteen of the thirty-eight states included in the current investigation are located in the South, it is necessary to control for this as a factor that contributes to homicide. South is a dichotomous variable with non-Southern states as the reference category. As identified by the United States Bureau of the Census, Southern states include Alabama, Arkansas, Delaware, Florida, Georgia, Kentucky, Louisiana, Maryland, Mississippi, North Carolina, Oklahoma, South Carolina, Tennessee, Texas, and Virginia.

Percent Metropolitan. Percent metropolitan is another socio demographic control factor found in studies of homicide (Land et al. 1990). Metropolitan areas are theorized to have higher rates of homicide because they are large areas that are densely populated.[8] Large and dense populations promote distrust and detachment because crime and predatory behavior are common interactions that accompany urban life. In this study, metropolitan population is operationalized as the percent of the population living in such areas.

Period Controls. Rates of homicide in the United States have fluctuated tremendously over recent decades. Data from the FBI's Uniform Crime Report shows that the average homicide rate for the period of 1991-1995 was 9.16 per 100,000 in the population. The rate of homicide decreased dramatically to 6.34 for the years 1996-2000, and declined slowly until it leveled off from 2001-2004 to an average rate of 5.6 (Bureau of Justice Statistics 2007). The relatively high rates of homicide during the early 1990s

---

[8] Metropolitan areas contain a core urban area of 50,000 or more and consist of one or more counties. They includes the counties containing the core urban area, as well as any adjacent counties that have a high degree of social and economic integration as measured by commuting to work (United States Department of Commerce Economics and Statistics Administration 1997).

have been attributed to larger proportions of young people in the population, the crack epidemic, and increased use of handguns, especially by juveniles and young adults (Blumstein, Rivara, and Rosenfeld 2000). By the mid 1990s the United States experienced sharp declines in homicides (Blumstein and Rosenfeld 2008; LaFree 1999). This decline in the homicide rate continued until the rate began to level off in 2000 and remained steady thereafter (Blumstein and Rosenfeld 2008). Levitt (2004) reviewed studies investigating declines in the homicide rate during the 1990s and concluded that increases in the number of police, increases in rates of incarceration, the receding crack epidemic, and the legalization of abortions played critical roles in explaining declines in homicides during this period. Ironically, one of the factors Levitt (2004) concluded did not contribute to the declining homicide rates during this period was the increased use of the death penalty during the 1990s.

The periods controlled in the current study are 1991-1995, 1996-2000, and 2000-2004. I control for these year groupings because they correspond to variation in the rate of decline for homicide trends. The period 1991-1995 had the highest average homicide rates and is, therefore, used as the reference category in the models. I expect that homicide rates will be significantly lower during the 1996-2000 and the 2001-2004 periods compared to the reference period of 1991-1995.

Analytical Strategy

In this study, I test several models that specify homicide rates as a function of the length of time death-row offenders wait for executions, controlling for other theoretical, sociodemographic, and time period factors. Using Ordinary Least Squares (OLS) regression has been a common way of examining aggregate relationships (Allison and Waterman 2002; Osgood 2000). However, when analyzing counts of relatively rare events such as homicides, the assumptions of homogeneity of the error variance is violated. Since crime rates would vary based on variations in populations, states with smaller populations would have larger predicted errors. In addition, because the state homicide counts are relatively small, it cannot be assumed that there is a normal error distribution. The lowest possible frequency for counts is zero, thus the error distribution are likely to be skewed. To avoid violating the assumptions of OLS regression, which can result in inconsistent and biased estimates of the coefficients, I use a negative binomial regression model which is a probability model that is more appropriate for analyzing counts of homicide (Osgood 2000). I specify the negative binomial model such that it includes the natural logarithm of the size of the population in the regression model and fixes its coefficient at one.[9] This allows for the analysis of rates of events rather than an analysis of counts of events (Osgood 2000). In addition, the state-year units are not independent cases because they are repeated measures within the same state. As such, the usual calculation of standard errors is biased and inconsistent. Consequently, I correct the standard errors for clustering by states.[10]

State-level data were pooled by state-year groups and increased the sample in the analysis from thirty-eight states to 114 state-year groups for the periods of 1991-1995, 1996-2000, and 2001-2004. Before estimating the negative binomial regression models, I examined the correlations

---

[9] In STATA I do this by using the offset option with ln (population size) as the offset variable.

[10] I do this in STATA by using the "cluster" command.

among the independent variables to assess problems of multicollinearity. Poverty, unemployment, and female headed households were highly correlated and as a result were combined into a scale of disadvantage with a Cronbach's alpha reliability statistic of .76. Another potential problem stemmed from the gap variables being highly correlated at -.8 or higher with the celerity dummy variable. To examine these correlations further, I reviewed the condition indices and variance-decomposition proportions from OLS models. These tests revealed no problems from multicollinearity in the parameter estimates. I use one-tailed tests of the significance of my variables since my hypotheses are directional. I also include the log of the total and race-specific populations as variables fixing the coefficient at one which changes the analyses to one of rates rather than counts, allowing for a more straightforward interpretation of my results.

Table 3.1 Operationalization of Dependent, Deterrence, and Sociodemographic Control Variables

VARIABLE NAME	DESCRIPTION
DEPENDENT VARIABLES (HOMICIDE COUNTS)	
Total Offenders	General Homicide Count: *total number of homicides in state-year groups*
White Offenders	White Homicide Count: *total number of white homicides in state-year groups*
Black Offenders	Black Homicide Count: *total number of black homicides in state-year groups*
DETERRENCE VARIABLES (CELERITY MEASURES)	
Offense Gap	Offense Celerity: *number of months from offense to execution [(execution year*12) + execution month]- [(offense year*12)+ offense month]*
Conviction Gap	Conviction Celerity: *number of months from conviction to execution ((execution year*12) + execution month)- ((conviction year*12)+ conviction month)*
Sentence Gap	Sentence Celerity: *number of months from sentence to execution ((execution year*12) + execution month)- ((sentence year*12)+ sentence month)*
Alive On Death Row	Average Time Alive on Death Row: *Average number of months prisoners under a sentence of death who were not executed have been on death row*
Alive On Death Row Dummy	Alive on death row dummy: *0=someone on death row in state-year group; 1=no one on death row in state-year group*
Celerity Dummy	Celerity Dummy: *0=execution in state 1=no execution in state*
(CERTAINTY MEASURES)	
Total Executions	Total Executions: *total number of executions in state during state-year group*
White Executions	White Executions: *total number of whites executed during state-year group*
Black Executions	Black Executions: total *number of Blacks executed during state-year group*

Table 3.1 Operationalization of Dependent, Deterrence, and Sociodemographic Control Variables (Continued)

VARIABLE NAME	DESCRIPTION
<u>SOCIODEMOGRAPHIC VARIABLES</u>	
Metropolitan	Percent Metropolitan: *percent of the state living in urban areas of 50,000 or more and consist of one or more counties*
Young Males	Percent Young Males: *percent males in state aged 16-34*
Young White Males	Percent Young White Males: *percent white males in state aged 15-34*
Young Black Males	Percent Young Black Males: *percent black males in state aged 15-34*
South	Dummy Variable for Southern Region: *0=non-Southern state; 1=Southern state*
Disadvantage	State Disadvantage scale: *mean of the z-scores of percent in state living in poverty, female-headed households, and who are unemployment*
White Disadvantage	White Disadvantage scale: *mean of the z-scores of percent of whites in state living in poverty, female-headed households, and who are unemployment*
Black Disadvantage	Black Disadvantage scale: *mean of the z-scores of percent of blacks in state living in poverty, female-headed households, and who are unemployment*
Total Population	Total Population: total state population
White Population	White Population: total population in a state that is white alone
Black Population	Black Population: total population in a state that is black or African American alone
<u>PERIOD VARIABLES</u>	
Time 1	1991-1995; *0=1996-2004; 1=1991-1995*
Time 2	1996-2000; *0=1991-1995; 1=1996-2000*
Time 3	2001-2004; *0=1991-1995; 1=2001-2004*

Chapter 4

A Description of the Data

The previous chapters highlighted the important contributions this study offers to the death penalty and deterrence theory literatures, reviewed the existing research on celerity as well as the other dimensions of punishment offered by deterrence theory, and explained the analytic strategy used in this study to better understand the role of celerity in executions. In this chapter, I present my descriptive results. Specifically, I present the means, standard deviations, and ranges of the variables employed in the models, and provide information on how long inmates wait prior to execution from the date of the offense, conviction and sentence by state-year groups.

Descriptive Results

Homicides. Table 4.1 presents means, standard deviations, and ranges of the dependent, independent, and control variables used in the analyses. Considering only states with the death penalty, in the years 1995, 2000, and 2004 there were 21,337, 14,237, and 15,279 homicides, respectively. There was an average of 326 homicides per 100,000 people among the state-year groups but counts ranged from a low of eight to a high of over 2,800.

Celerity in Executions. Table 4.1 illustrates, that on average, offenders waited 151.87 months (12.66 years) from the time of committing a capital homicide to execution. The offense-to-execution gap is obviously longer than the conviction-to-execution gap which is 138.12 months (11.51 years). The shortest gap is the wait for execution subsequent to sentencing which averages 128.57 months (10.71 years). This suggests that over one year passes between offenses and convictions for capital offenses, and about ten months pass between convictions and sentences to death. The celerity dummy variable has a mean of .37 suggesting that about one-third of the state-year groups did not have an execution during the study periods. The average time alive variable has a mean of eighty-one suggesting that on average, the non-executed capital offenders spend nearly eighty-one months (6.75 years) on death row. This average wait is shorter than the wait from sentencing to execution because it includes prisoners that died or were exonerated before their capital sentences were carried out. The average time alive on death row dummy has a mean of .06 and shows that only a small portion of the state-year groups did not have anyone on death row. In fact, only seven state-year groups failed to place anyone on death row during the periods examined in this study.

Certainty in Executions. As a reminder, certainty is measured as the total number of executions during the period. Table 4.1 also shows that death penalty states carried out an average of seven executions during the state-year groups in the study. Executions ranged from a minimum of zero to a maximum of 135 across state-year groups.

Table 4.1. Descriptive Statistics for Homicides, Deterrence Variables, Sociodemographic Variables, and Period Variables.

VARIABLE NAME	MEAN	STANDARD DEVIATION	MINIMUM	MAXIMUM
Dependent Variable				
Homicide Offenders	325.59	408.95	8	2823
Deterrence Variables				
Offense Celerity	151.87	84.52	35	263
Conviction Celerity	138.12	75.75	26	242
Sentence Celerity	128.57	72.66	21	242
Celerity Dummy	0.37	0.48	0	1
Alive On Death Row	80.83	39.80	3.96	168
Alive Dummy	0.06	0.24	0	1
Total Executions	6.98	18.14	1	135
Sociodemographic Variables				
Disadvantage Scale	.01	0.81	-1.55	2.56
Female-Headed Households	11.14	2.10	7.68	16.97
Poverty	12.19	3.51	5.64	22.34
Unemployed	3.74	.59	2.45	5.62
Metropolitan	69.20	19.86	23.90	100
Young Males	14.39	1.09	11.83	17.33
South	0.39	0.49	0	1
Total Population	6,108,396	6,383,957	453,588	33,871,648

N=111

A closer look at the distribution indicates that Texas carried out the most executions followed by Virginia (52) and Oklahoma (45) (not shown). Connecticut, Kansas, New Hampshire, New Jersey, New York, and South Dakota, however, did not execute anyone during the years of the study (not shown).

Sociodemographic Control Variables. Structural disadvantage is a scale which includes poverty, unemployment, and the percent living in female-headed households. Table 4.1 presents the descriptive information for the scale and its components. As shown, the scale for disadvantage ranges from a low of -1.55 to a high of 2.56. The state-year groups have an average of 11.14 percent of their population living in female-headed households. A further perusal of the distribution of the data indicates that from 1991-1995 South Dakota and Idaho (not shown) had the lowest levels of female-headed households with less than eight percent of its population living in such households. By 2001-2004, rates of female-headed households peaked in Louisiana and Mississippi (not shown) to over sixteen percent of its population living in such households.

States with the death penalty differ considerably regarding the percentage of the population living below the poverty level. On average state-year groups had 12.19 percent of their populations living below the poverty level. However, states ranged from less than six percent (Connecticut and New Hampshire) poor to highs of over twenty percent (Mississippi). In addition, on average, state-year groups had 3.74 percent of their populations unemployed with rates in the state-year groups ranging from to 2.45 percent (Nebraska) to 5.6 percent (Louisiana). Mississippi (4.96%) and New Mexico (4.93%) also had relatively high rates of unemployment, while New Hampshire (2.65 %) and Delaware (2.69) had relatively low levels of unemployment across state-year groups (not shown).

Beyond disadvantage, the state-year groups in this study, on average, are over two-thirds (69.2%) metropolitan although this varies tremendously and ranges from a low of nearly twenty-four percent metropolitan in Montana during 1991-1995 to a high of 100 percent in New Jersey for each study period. Young males accounts for roughly fourteen percent of the population over the state-year groups and this variable ranges from nearly twelve percent to just over seventeen percent. Fifteen of the thirty-eight states in the analysis are located in the South accounting for roughly thirty-nine percent of the sample.[11]

Variations in Homicide by State and Years

To provide a better sense of the distribution of homicides across the cases, Table 4.2 shows the rank ordering (high to low) of homicides by state and year. For comparative purposes, the table reports rates per 100,000 rather than simple counts. Average homicide rates in 1995, 2000, and 2004 among death penalty states were 6.32, 4.01, and 4.78 per 100,000 persons, respectively. Thus, homicide rates declined substantially from 1995 to 2000 and subsequently increased slightly from 200 to 2004.

---

[11]The fifteen states located in the South that have a legal provision for the death penalty throughout the duration of the study period include: Alabama, Arkansas, Delaware, Florida, Georgia, Kentucky, Louisiana, Maryland, Mississippi, North Carolina, Oklahoma, South Carolina, Tennessee, Texas, and Virginia. The states classified as Southern by the U.S. Bureau of the Census remained the same throughout the study.

Table 4.2. State Homicide Rates by Year

State[12]	1995 Homicide Rate	State	2000 Homicide Rate	State	2004 Homicide Rate
Louisiana	12.04	South Carolina	10.19	Louisiana	11.03
South Carolina	11.39	Louisiana	9.69	South Carolina	10.19
Arkansas	10.72	Tennessee	6.86	Arizona	7.44
Arizona	10.53	North Carolina	6.81	New Mexico	7.44
Nevada	10.32	Maryland	6.33	Tennessee	7.36
Texas	9.60	Arkansas	6.06	Nevada	7.06
Maryland	9.35	Mississippi	6.01	Maryland	6.67
Oklahoma	9.25	Virginia	5.98	Texas	6.37
North Carolina	9.25	Texas	5.67	North Carolina	6.04
California	9.09	Oklahoma	5.36	Oklahoma	5.94
Georgia	8.78	Arizona	5.26	Mississippi	5.91
Tennessee	8.35	California	4.71	Virginia	5.73
Missouri	7.88	New Mexico	4.62	Colorado	5.58
Alabama	7.45	Missouri	4.59	Missouri	5.51
Virginia	7.05	Georgia	4.50	California	5.49

Note: Rates are per 100,000 persons

---

[12] States with identical homicide rates are listed in alphabetical order.

Table 4.2. State Homicide Rates by Year (Continued)

State	1995 Homicide Rate	State	2000 Homicide Rate	State	2004 Homicide Rate
Illinois	6.54	Nevada	4.50	Arkansas	5.41
Mississippi	6.49	Pennsylvania	4.32	Georgia	5.41
New Mexico	6.40	Delaware	4.08	Pennsylvania	4.75
Colorado	6.22	Alabama	4.05	Kentucky	4.63
Florida	5.66	New York	3.56	Alabama	4.45
Idaho	5.66	Indiana	3.24	Idaho	4.17
Pennsylvania	5.61	Washington	3.21	Montana	4.00
Kentucky	5.37	Colorado	2.95	New Jersey	3.77
Washington	4.91	Connecticut	2.73	Indiana	3.73
Oregon	4.86	New Jersey	2.70	Washington	3.53
Utah	4.82	Illinois	2.46	Utah	3.34
New York	4.77	Ohio	2.46	Ohio	3.32
Indiana	4.35	Wyoming	2.43	Kansas	3.25
Ohio	4.17	Oregon	2.02	Oregon	3.19
New Jersey	4.10	Utah	1.84	New York	2.94

Note: Rates are per 100,000 persons

Table 4.2. State Homicide Rates by Year (Continued)

State	1995 Homicide Rate	State	2000 Homicide Rate	State	2004 Homicide Rate
Connecticut	3.62	Kansas	1.71	Illinois	2.88
Montana	2.38	Nebraska	1.64	Wyoming	2.32
South Dakota	1.87	Idaho	1.31	South Dakota	1.93
Wyoming	1.76	Kentucky	1.26	Connecticut	1.82
Delaware	1.32	New Hampshire	1.13	Delaware	1.66
New Hampshire	1.17	South Dakota	1.06	Nebraska	1.58
Nebraska	0.89	Montana	0.89	New Hampshire	0.94
Kansas	--	Florida	--	Florida	--
Mean Homicide Rate	**6.32**		**4.01**		**4.78**

Note: Rates are per 100,000 persons.

Averaging the years 1995, 2000, and 2004 Louisiana (10.92) and South Carolina (10.59) had the highest homicide rates. According to deterrence theory, these states would be expected to have the longest waits prior to executions. However, this is not the case; neither Louisiana nor South Carolina are among the ten least celeritous states (see Tables 4.3, 4.4, and 4.5 below). Conversely, Nebraska (1.37) and New Hampshire (1.08), with the lowest homicide rates would be expected to have the shortest waits for executions. Nevertheless, Nebraska, is one of the least celeritous states for the periods 1991-1995 and 1996-2000 and did not execute anyone from 2001-2004.

Moreover, New Hampshire had the lowest average homicide rate of 1.08 although New Hampshire did not execute anyone during the entire study period. A more detailed discussion of waits to executions by state-year groups will follow below

Waits from Offense to Execution

Table 4.3 lists all states with capital punishment during the study periods ordered from least to most celeritous from offense to execution across year groups. There is a wide range in how long offenders wait after their offenses for executions across jurisdictions. Prisoners executed between 1991-1995 waited an average of 148.08 (12.34 years) months from offense to execution. This wait increased to 153.17 months (12.76 years) for those executed between 1996-2000, and then increased again to 162.35 months (13.53 years) for 2001-2004. Table 4.3 also shows that, in 1991-1995 capital offenders in Montana, Utah, Illinois, and Nebraska had waited an average of over 200 months after their offenses to be executed. Montana had the longest waits with capital offenders waiting 256 months (21.33 years) from offense to execution.

By 1996-2000 six states (Tennessee, California, Alabama, Arizona, Kentucky, and Florida) had average waits of over 200 months. Tennessee had the longest waits during this period, with prisoners waiting about 247 months (20.58 years).

California was the least celeritous during 2001-2004; prisoners had waited an average of 263 months (21.92 years) after their offenses, prior to being executed. During this same period, Georgia, Mississippi, and Ohio also had waits longer than 200 months. Overall, averaging the three periods for each state, California (214.06 months) and Alabama (191.9 months) were the least celeritous states (not shown).

Table 4.3 also shows that Idaho (37 months) and Maryland (44 months) were the two most celeritous states during 1991-1995, with waits of less than four years. From 1996-2000 Washington and Nevada had the shortest waits during the period. Prisoners in Washington waited only thirty-five months (2.92 years) to be executed. Washington, from 2001-2004, had the shortest waits prior to execution averaging forty months. Across the three periods, Washington has the shortest average waits from offenses to executions, with capital offenders waiting almost fifty-six months (4.65 years) to be executed. Idaho (37 months) murderers were executed within five years after their offenses from 1991-1995, but Idaho did not execute from 1996-2004. No other jurisdictions averaged five years or fewer between the crime and executions. Of note, Alabama, California, and Florida were consistently ranked in the top ten least celeritous states across the three periods and Delaware, Virginia, and Washington were

Table 4.3. Average Number of Months from Offense to Executions by Year Groups and State

STATE	1991-1995 Months	STATE	1996-2000 Months	STATE	2001-2004 Months
Montana	256.00	Tennessee	247.00	California	263.00
Utah	219.00	California	216.17	Georgia	255.77
Illinois	211.33	Alabama	213.82	Mississippi	211.00
Nebraska	207.00	Arizona	211.06	Ohio	202.43
Georgia	177.50	Kentucky	208.50	Maryland	199.00
Indiana	168.00	Florida	205.93	Alabama	198.14
Alabama	163.75	Nebraska	199.00	Indiana	192.75
California	163.00	Illinois	187.80	Florida	187.89
Florida	159.91	South Carolina	178.70	New Mexico	184.00
Arizona	155.50	Oklahoma	162.21	Oklahoma	158.91
Arkansas	154.89	Louisiana	160.50	Missouri	156.47
Wyoming	152.00	Indiana	159.00	Delaware	144.50
Pennsylvania	150.00	North Carolina	157.25	Arkansas	143.33
South Carolina	149.00	Arkansas	154.25	North Carolina	140.39
Oklahoma	144.20	Texas	154.12	Texas	139.46
Missouri	144.17	Georgia	154.00	South Carolina	138.57

Table 4.3. Average Number of Months from Offense to Executions by Year Groups and State (Continued)

STATE	1991-1995 Months	STATE	1996-2000 Months	STATE	2001-2004 Months
Texas	140.88	Missouri	153.31	Louisiana	130.00
Louisiana	133.33	Pennsylvania	149.00	Virginia	85.77
North Carolina	129.00	Colorado	135.00	Nevada	75.67
Virginia	122.50	Maryland	129.50	Washington	40.00
Washington	92.50	Delaware	117.00	Arizona	-
Delaware	79.40	Montana	115.00	Colorado	-
Maryland	44.00	Utah	112.50	Connecticut	-
Idaho	37.00	Ohio	110.00	Idaho	-
Colorado	-	Nevada	103.33	Illinois	-
Connecticut	-	Virginia	100.37	Kansas	-
Kansas	-	Oregon	59.50	Kentucky	-
Kentucky	-	Washington	35.00	Montana	-
Mississippi	-	Connecticut	-	Nebraska	-
Nevada	-	Idaho	-	New Hampshire	-
New Hampshire	-	Kansas	-	New Jersey	-
New Jersey	-	Mississippi	-	New York	-
New Mexico	-	New Hampshire	-	North Dakota	-
New York	-	New Jersey	-	Oregon	-
North Dakota	-	New Mexico	-	Pennsylvania	-

Table 4.3. Average Number of Months from Offense to Executions by Year Groups and State (Continued)

STATE	1991-1995 Months	STATE	1996-2000 Months	STATE	2001-2004 Months
Ohio	-	New York	-	South Dakota	-
Oregon	-	North Dakota	-	Tennessee	-
South Dakota	-	South Dakota	-	Utah	-
Tennessee	-	Vermont	-	Vermont	-
Vermont	-	Wisconsin	-	Wisconsin	-
Wisconsin	-	Wyoming	-	Wyoming	-
Mean Months	**148.08**		**153.17**		**162.35**
Total Executions	170.00		370.00		261.00

ranked among the top ten most celeritous states across the periods under study.

Waits from Conviction to Execution

Table 4.4 shows the waits from conviction to execution for death penalty state-year groups ordered from least to most celeritous. Overall, waits from conviction to execution are increasing. Offenders executed between 1991 and 1995 waited an average of 132.72 months (11.06 years) from conviction to execution. This increased to 138.13 months (11.51 years) during the 1996-2000 period, and by the 2001-2004 period, the average number of months offenders had waited was 143.51 (11.96 years). Waits from conviction to execution varied from a low of twenty-six months (2.17 years) in Maryland from 1991-1995 to a high of 242 months (20.17 years) in Montana for the same period. By the period 1996-2000, Tennessee had the longest wait from conviction to execution and prisoners waited over 227 months (18.92 years) followed by Kentucky where offenders waited 197.50 months (16.46 years) after a conviction for their execution. The most recent years included in the analyses had the fewest states that executed and offenders waited the longest in Georgia (224 months) followed by Mississippi (202.50 months).

Table 4.4 also shows that the most celeritous states during 1991-1995 were Maryland (26 months) and Idaho (27months); both states executed offenders in less than 2.5 years on average. During the 1996-2000 period, Washington was the most celeritous, executing offenders in thirty-two months, followed by Oregon where waits for executions after convictions lasted an average of forty-three months (3.58 years). Washington was also the most celeritous state during the 2001-2004 period with offenders

Table 4.4. Average Number of Months from Conviction to Execution by Year Groups and State

STATE	1991-1995 Months	STATE	1996-2000 Months	STATE	2001-2004 Months
Montana	242.00	Tennessee	227.00	Georgia	224.00
Utah	212.00	Kentucky	197.50	Mississippi	202.50
Nebraska	197.00	Arizona	195.50	California	195.50
Illinois	178.67	California	194.67	Ohio	188.79
Indiana	162.00	Nebraska	189.50	Alabama	182.71
Alabama	151.50	Alabama	184.73	Indiana	177.75
Wyoming	148.00	Florida	171.36	Florida	174.56
Florida	145.45	Illinois	165.40	New Mexico	174.00
South Carolina	143.50	South Carolina	165.10	Maryland	158.00
Pennsylvania	143.00	North Carolina	148.50	Oklahoma	147.27
Georgia	142.83	Indiana	148.25	Missouri	140.80
Arizona	140.50	Oklahoma	147.88	Arkansas	137.67
California	140.00	Georgia	144.33	Delaware	127.50
Oklahoma	130.80	Louisiana	143.25	North Carolina	122.44
Missouri	130.42	Texas	139.36	Texas	120.88

Table 4.4. Average Number of Months from Conviction to Execution by Year Groups and State (Continued)

STATE	1991-1995 Months	STATE	1996-2000 Months	STATE	2001-2004 Months
Texas	126.27	Arkansas	134.67	South Carolina	120.57
Louisiana	120.67	Pennsylvania	132.00	Louisiana	114.00
North Carolina	119.20	Missouri	131.03	Nevada	66.67
Virginia	110.61	Colorado	123.00	Virginia	55.54
Arkansas	110.56	Maryland	123.00	Washington	39.00
Washington	84.00	Montana	109.00	Arizona	-
Delaware	53.40	Utah	109.00	Colorado	-
Idaho	27.00	Delaware	105.50	Connecticut	-
Maryland	26.00	Ohio	102.00	Idaho	-
Colorado	-	Virginia	88.12	Illinois	-
Connecticut	-	Nevada	73.00	Kansas	-
Kansas	-	Oregon	43.00	Kentucky	-
Kentucky	-	Washington	32.00	Montana	-
Mississippi	-	Connecticut	-	Nebraska	-

Table 4.4. Average Number of Months from Conviction to Execution by Year Groups and State (Continued)

STATE	1991-1995 Months	STATE	1996-2000 Months	STATE	2001-2004 Months
Nevada	-	Idaho	-	New Hampshire	-
New Hampshire	-	Kansas	-	New Jersey	-
New Jersey	-	Mississippi	-	New York	-
New Mexico	-	New Hampshire	-	Oregon	-
New York	-	New Jersey	-	Pennsylvania	-
Ohio	-	New Mexico	-	South Dakota	-
Oregon	-	New York	-	Tennessee	-
South Dakota	-	South Dakota	-	Utah	-
Tennessee	-	Wyoming	-	Wyoming	-
Mean Months	**132.72**		**138.13**		**143.51**
Total Executions	170		370		261

waiting an average of thirty-nine months after their convictions for their executions. In fact, among the states that executed during all three periods, Washington had the shortest average waits from conviction to execution with offenders having an average wait of 51.66 months (4.31 years). Finally, I should note that states were quite variable over time in the amount of wait between convictions and executions. For example, Florida was the only state to be in the top ten least celeritous jurisdictions in all three periods.

Waits from Sentence to Execution

As Table 4.5 shows, waits rose and fell across the time periods under study. From 1991-1995 prisoners waited an average of 127 months after sentencing to be executed. This wait increased to 130 months during the 1996-2000 period and then fell to 129 months from 2001-2004. Those executed in Montana between 1991-1995 had the longest waits from sentence, to execution, with an average wait of 242 months (20.17 years), followed by Utah with an average wait of 212 months (17.67 years).

Conversely, Idaho had the shortest waits during 1991-1995 with prisoners waiting twenty-one months (1.75 years) on average to be executed. Maryland also had relatively short waits to executions after sentencing with offenders waiting an average of twenty-six months (2.17 years). Table 4.5, also shows that during the period 1996-2000, Tennessee had the longest wait from sentence to execution, averaging 227 months (18.92) followed by Kentucky with 196.50 months (16.38 years). During this same period, Washington had the most celeritous executions, with offenders waiting thirty-two months (2.67 years) before their executions; over sixteen years shorter

Table 4.5. Average Number of Months from Sentence to Execution by Year Groups and State

STATE	1991-1995 Months	STATE	1996-2000 Months	STATE	2001-2004 Months
Montana	242.00	Tennessee	227.00	Georgia	218.31
Utah	212.00	Kentucky	196.50	Ohio	188.21
Nebraska	195.00	California	194.63	Alabama	174.71
Illinois	174.80	Nebraska	187.50	Mississippi	166.00
Indiana	161.00	Arizona	179.08	California	165.50
Florida	149.40	Alabama	175.23	Florida	163.44
South Carolina	143.50	Florida	173.55	Maryland	158.00
Pennsylvania	142.00	Illinois	154.38	Oklahoma	145.53
Alabama	141.00	South Carolina	148.83	Missouri	139.80
California	136.00	Indiana	147.50	Indiana	139.25
Oklahoma	133.33	Louisiana	143.25	Delaware	127.50
Arizona	133.00	Pennsylvania	132.00	Texas	120.77
North Carolina	124.50	Texas	128.55	South Carolina	120.57
Texas	123.49	Missouri	126.74	North Carolina	120.00
Louisiana	119.33	Oklahoma	124.03	Louisiana	114.00
Georgia	118.13	Colorado	123.00	Arkansas	95.67
Wyoming	116.00	Maryland	120.50	Nevada	65.57

Table 4.5. Average Number of Months from Sentence to Execution by Year Groups and State (Continued)

STATE	1991-1995 Months	STATE	1996-2000 Months	STATE	2001-2004 Months
Missouri	106.19	North Carolina	117.42	New Mexico	65.00
Virginia	102.46	Georgia	111.00	Virginia	51.46
Washington	83.50	Montana	109.00	Washington	34.00
Arkansas	78.83	Utah	106.50	Arizona	-
Delaware	55.38	Ohio	102.00	Colorado	-
Maryland	26.00	Delaware	97.78	Connecticut	-
Idaho	21.00	Arkansas	97.50	Idaho	-
Colorado	-	Virginia	84.15	Illinois	-
Connecticut	-	Nevada	71.00	Kansas	-
Kansas	-	Oregon	42.00	Kentucky	-
Kentucky	-	Washington	32.00	Montana	-
Mississippi	-	Connecticut	-	Nebraska	-
Nevada	-	Idaho	-	New Hampshire	-
New Hampshire	-	Kansas	-	New Jersey	-
New Jersey	-	Mississippi	-	New York	-
New Mexico	-	New Hampshire	-	Oregon	-

Table 4.5. Average Number of Months from Sentence to Execution by Year Groups and State (Continued)

STATE	1991-1995 Months	STATE	1996-2000 Months	STATE	2001-2004 Months
New York	-	New Jersey	-	Pennsylvania	-
Ohio	-	New Mexico	-	South Dakota	-
Oregon	-	New York	-	Tennessee	-
South Dakota	-	South Dakota	-	Utah	-
Tennessee	-	Wyoming	-	Wyoming	-
Mean Months	**126.58**		**130.45**		**128.66**
Total Executions	170		370		261

than what capital offenders waited for executions in Tennessee. Ten of the thirty-eight states did not execute during this period, four fewer states compared to the 1991-1996 period.

During the 2001-2004 period, Georgia's death sentenced inmates had waited the longest before executions, averaging 218 months (18.17 years) followed by Ohio with an average wait of 188 months (15.67 years) from sentence to execution. Similar to the 1996-2000 period, Washington had the shortest waits from sentences to executions. Washington's executions took place, on average, 36 months (3 years) after sentencing. This most recent period in the study had the most number of states that did not execute anyone. In fact, from 2001-2004, of the thirty-eight states with capital punishment, eighteen of them did not execute anyone. Four states were in the slowest-to-execution jurisdictions in all three periods: Alabama, California, Florida, and Indiana. As noted, the state of Washington is one of the quickest to execute after sentencing offenders to death. Beyond that, however, there is not much consistency to where states fell in the rank ordering of most to least celeritous executing state over time.

Waits for Executions Are Becoming Longer

Tables 4.3, 4.4, and 4.5 indicate that waits on death row are becoming longer. As a whole, averaging the offense, conviction, and sentence celerity measures, waits for executions have indeed become longer. For executions taking place between 1991 and 1995, the average wait had been 135.79 months (11.48 years). Waits increased to 140.58 months (11.72 years) for the 1996-2000 period, and increased again to 144.84 months (12.07 years) during the

2001-2004 period. Among the sixteen states that executed during all three periods, only Indiana decreased waits across the three years and across the three different celerity measures. From 1991-1995, averaging the offense, conviction, and sentence gaps, Indiana's capital offenders waited an average of 161 months (13.42 years) prior to executions. This wait decreased to 147.5 months (12.29 years) by the 1996- 2000 period, and by 2001-2004 those inmates executed in Indiana had waited 139.25 months (11.6 years) prior to executions.

In addition, on the surface, there does not appear to be a relationship between longer waits for executions and homicide rates. The states with the longest waits prior to executions do not coincide with the states with the highest homicide rates, and conversely, the states with the shortest waits prior to execution do not correspond to the states with the lowest homicide rates. For example, as Table 4.2 illustrates, Louisiana and South Carolina have the highest homicide rates in 1995, 2000, and 2004. According to deterrence theory, these should be associated with longer waits prior to executions. However, the tables displaying the average offense, conviction, and sentence celerity gaps (Tables 4.3, 4.4, and 4.5) from high to low by state-year groups indicate that Louisiana is not among the top five states with the longest (or shortest) waits on death row despite having the highest homicide rate in 1995 and 2004, and the second highest in 2000. South Carolina, also had a relatively high homicide rate, yet like Louisiana, its ranking in the celerity tables never reaches the top five.

Similar patterns exist for the states with the lowest homicide rates. As the homicide data in Table 4.2 show, New Hampshire and Nebraska are the two states with the lowest average homicide rates for the years 1995, 2000, and 2004. According to deterrence theory, New Hampshire and Nebraska should have relatively short waits on death row since they have the lowest overall homicide rates. However, Tables 4.3, 4.4, and 4.5 show that New Hampshire did not administer any executions, a finding in stark contrast to deterrence theory predictions. In addition, Nebraska was among the top ten states with the longest waits from offense and conviction to execution, during 1991-1995 and 1996-2000. Furthermore, during 2001-2004, Nebraska did not execute anyone. Put together, the state data on homicides and waits for executions do not correspond to one another in the manner hypothesized by deterrence theory. The states with the shortest or longest waits until executions fail to correspond with the lowest and highest homicide rates.

Bivariate Correlations

Table 4.6 presents the bivariate correlations of the dependent and independent variables used in the general models. As illustrated in Table 4.6, the deterrence measures with the exception of the celerity dummy variable and the average time alive on death row dummy variable are positively correlated with homicides. The strength of the correlation coefficients indicates that there is only a moderate association between homicides and certainty of executions and a weak association with the average time spent on death row. Nonetheless, state-year groups that have higher homicide rates also tend to have more executions and inmates wait longer to be executed. The sociodemographic variables are also positively correlated with homicides. The coefficients indicate that the percent metropolitan, disadvantage, young males and Southern region are moderately correlated with homicide rates. The period variables however, have a weak relationship with homicides although time period one is positively correlated

Table 4.6. Bivariate Correlation Matrix of Dependent and Independent Variables

	V1	V2	V3	V4	V5	V6	V7	V8	V9	V10	V11	V12	V13	V14	V15
Homicides (V1)	1														
Certainty (V2)	.376	1													
Offense Gap (V3)	.296	.246	1												
Conviction Gap (V4)	.216	.166	.884	1											
Sentence Gap (V5)	.274	.252	.959	.901	1										
Celerity Dummy (V6)	-.253	-.296	-.838	-.804	-.842	1									
Avg. Time Alive (V7)	.084	.028	.333	.353	.363	-.283	1								
Avg Alive Dummy (V8)	-.099	-.098	-.228	-.216	-.226	.262	-.43	1							
Metropolitan (V9)	.459	.133	.054	.03	.075	-.132	.042	-.149	1						
Disadvantage (V10)	.296	.113	.214	.132	.135	-.132	.075	-.167	-.039	1					
Young Males (V11)	.390	.178	.131	.102	.146	-.191	-.126	-.007	.258	.039	1				
South (V12)	.128	.333	.314	.297	.303	-.379	.123	-.130	.052	.427	.115	1			
Time 1 (V13)	.144	-.094	.509	-.054	.000	-.026	-.253	.131	.007	.037	.509	.026	1		
Time 2 (V14)	-.087	.103	.11	.158	.141	-.145	-.046	-.105	-.027	.004	.131	-.013	-.500	1	
Time 3 (V15)	-.056	-.010	-.109	-.105	-.141	.172	.300	-.026	.020	.033	-.640	-.013	-.500	-.500	1

with homicides while time periods two and three are negatively correlated with homicides.

The variables in the models were assessed for multicollinearity by examining the multiple correlations of each independent variable regressed on all the other independent variables. The assessment for multicollinearity revealed that the celerity variables were highly correlated (Agresti and Finlay, 1997) with one another.[13] For example, the offense gap is correlated with the conviction gap at .884 and the correlation among the offense gap and sentence gap is even higher (.959). A similar pattern exists for the conviction gap and the sentence gap which is correlated at .901. These correlations indicate that the three variables are overlapping and should not be included simultaneously in models of homicide.

---

[13] A coefficient of .60 or higher is the criteria used.

Chapter 5

Quicker Executions Fail to Impact Homicide Rates

The previous chapter provided descriptive statistics for the variables and provided state-year information on the celerity gaps investigated in this study. In this chapter, I present the negative binomial regression results that examine the effects of various measures of celerity on state homicide rates to determine whether how long offenders wait before being executed influences murder rates.

To reiterate briefly, there have been only two empirical studies tackling the issue of celerity and they reached contradictory conclusions. Bailey (1980) hypothesized a positive relationship between longer waits prior to executions and state homicide rates. He tested his hypotheses using Ordinary Least-Squares (OLS) regression and concluded that celeritous executions fail to deter murders. His celerity measures were not significantly related to homicides and his findings failed to support the propositions offered by deterrence theory.

More recently, Shepherd (2004) addressed the issue of celerity again by examining the effect of waits on death row for deterring several types of murders. Shepherd (2004) uses OLS to test for the effects of the length of death row waits on six types of murders. She finds, on average, that one less murder is committed for every 2.75-year reduction in the expected death row wait. Furthermore, executions serve to reduce murders for both whites and blacks, as well as for intimate killings, and "crimes of passion." From these results, Shepherd concludes that lengthy stays on death row diminish the deterrent value of capital punishment. Her results support the deterrence proposition. With only two studies having tackled the issue and coming to different conclusions, more research is needed to shed light on the role that celerity in executions plays for deterring killings.

In line with deterrence theory, this study hypothesizes that shorter waits prior to executions are negatively associated with homicide rates. Put differently, I expect that states that execute capital offenders more swiftly will have significantly lower homicide rates compared to states that take longer to execute. To test the hypotheses offered in Chapter 3, I estimate negative binomial regression models to examine whether the length of time an offender waits from the offense, the conviction, or the sentence prior to execution impacts state homicide rates after controlling for certainty in executions, sociodemographic factors, and time periods.

Effect of Various Celerity Measures on State Homicide Rates

Prior studies of celerity focus on the gaps in time between sentencing and executions (Bailey, 1980 and Shepherd, 2004) and convictions and execution (Bailey, 1980). In this assessment, I consider both the previously considered gaps (i.e. the sentence and conviction gaps) as well as the gap between the offense and the execution in negative binomial regression models.

Table 5.1 presents the results of the negative binomial regression models. Models 1, 2, and 3 respectively show the effects of the offense, conviction, and sentence celerity measures on state homicide rates. The values in the tables are the regression coefficients and standard errors (in parentheses). As illustrated in Table 5.1, the coefficients for the celerity measures across the models are -.00004 (offense), .00037 (conviction), and -.00062 (sentence), respectively. Overall, the coefficients indicate that the waits before executions, however measured, do not significantly impact homicide rates. A one unit increase in any of the celerity measures is associated with less than a .1 percent decrease in the homicide rate and this effect is insignificant across the models.[14]

Time from Offense to Execution. With regard to Model 1, the coefficient representing the offense to execution gap in Table 5.1 is -.00004. The effect is insignificant and illustrates that every month waited prior to execution is associated with a .004 percent decrease in state homicide rates. The celerity dummy variable is also insignificant. The variables time spent on death row and time spent on death row dummy also fail to significantly reduce homicide rates. The time alive on death row coefficient is positive (.00035), and the time alive on death row dummy coefficient is negative (-.38109) but neither is significantly associated with homicides. The certainty

---

[14] The unit change is calculated by subtracting e^b from one and then multiplying it by 100. (Long 1997: 225). Using the example of the sentence gap from Table 5.1, the unit change is calculated as ($e^{-.001}$- 1)*100 = .10. Using this formula allows for a more straightforward interpretation of the negative binomial regression coefficients. Essentially, this indicates a percentage change in the outcome (homicides) for every one unit change in the explanatory variable.

coefficient (.00032) is positive but this coefficient is also not statistically significant. Again, the effects of all of the deterrence measures in Model 1 are insignificant, and as a group, the directions of the coefficients, are not consistent with deterrence theory predictions.

The sociodemographic variables in Model 1, with the exception of young males, have significant negative effects on homicide rates. The coefficient representing metropolitan is .00635 and indicates that for every percentage increase in the metropolitan population, state-year groups experience a slight .6 percent increase in the homicide rate. Disadvantage, is also a predictor of homicide among the sociodemographic factors. The coefficient of .26086 suggests that for every unit increase in levels of disadvantage, state-year groups experience almost a thirty percent increase in homicides. The coefficient representing the effect of Southern region (.35608) also significantly predicts homicide rates such that states located in the South have homicide rates that are nearly forty-three percent higher than non-Southern states. Young males is the only sociodemographic variable that fails to predict homicide rates. Overall, the sociodemographic variables are in their predicted directions, and the results indicate that three of the four are better predictors of homicide rates than the deterrence measures in the model.

Only the coefficient for time period 2 (-.36490), capturing the years from 1996-2000, is significantly associated with homicide rates. Compared to time period 1 (1991-1995), homicide rates were thirty percent lower during time period 2 (1996-2000). Unlike time period 2 (1996-2000), time period 3 (2001-2004) was not significantly related to homicide rates.

Table 5.1. Negative Binomial Regression Models of Homicide Offenders on Deterrence, Sociodemographic, and Time Period Variables

	Model 1 Offense Gap	Model 2 Conviction Gap	Model 3 Sentence Gap
DETERRENCE VARIABLES			
Celerity	-.00004	.00037	-.00062
	(.00094)	(.00106)	(.00133)
Celerity Dummy	-.11872	-.06748	-.11819
	(.21239)	(.20674)	(.23614)
Time Alive on Death Row	.00035	.00024	.00056
	(.00129)	(.00130)	(.00134)
Time Alive on Death Row Dummy	-.38109	-.38810	-.36658
	(.22605)	(.22710)	(.22928)
Certainty (Total Executions)	.00032	.00043	.00036
	(.00275)	(.00272)	(.00279)
SOCIODEMOGRAPHIC VARIABLES			
Metropolitan	.00635*	.00638*	.00641**
	(.00250)	(.00255)	(.00246)
Disadvantage	.26086***	.25867***	.26299***
	(.06694)	(.06294)	(.06297)
Young Males	.09037	.08899	.09095
	(.05166)	(.05213)	(.05122)

Table 5.1. Negative Binomial Regression Models of Homicide Offenders on Deterrence, Sociodemographic, and Time Period Variables (Continued)

	Model 1 Offense Gap	Model 2 Conviction Gap	Model 3 Sentence Gap
Southern Region	.35608*	.35802**	.35225**
	(.12596)	(.12039)	(.12334)
TIME PERIODS			
Time 2 (1996-2000)	-.36490***	-.37306***	-.36006***
	(.09898)	(.10486)	(.09939)
Time 3 (2001-2004)	-.19237	-.19862	-.19510
	(.14363)	(.14880)	(.13768)
CONSTANT	-11.64956***	-11.67271***	-11.60872***
	(.78572)	(.79099)	(.77940)
Wald χ^2 (DF=11) N=111	186.04	187.32	183.69

Note: Standard errors are in the parentheses. *p<.05, **p<.01, ***p<.001 (one-tailed)

The pattern for the time periods is consistent with homicide data showing that state homicide rates declined during the 1990s and then leveled off and remained steady through the early years of the 2000 millennium (Blumstein and Rosenfeld, 2008).

Time from Conviction to Execution. Table 5.1, shows the results of the negative binomial regression model testing the effect of the conviction gap on state homicide rates. The conviction gap coefficient (.00037) is positive although insignificant. In addition, the coefficients representing the celerity dummy (-.06748), time alive on death row (.00024) and time alive on death row dummy (-.38810) variables are insignificant. The positive coefficient for certainty in executions (.00043) also fails to significantly impact homicide rates. In fact, of the five deterrence variables in Model 2, three of them (celerity dummy, time alive on death row dummy, and certainty) are in the opposite direction of what deterrence theory proposes. Overall, the model does not support deterrence theory propositions regarding the role of celerity in executions. The fact that none of the deterrence measures are significant suggests that the wait from conviction to execution is unrelated to state homicide rates. This is consistent with a long line of deterrence research.

The coefficients representing the sociodemographic variables in Model 2 are very similar to the coefficients shown in Model 1. The coefficient for metropolitan population (.00638) changes only slightly across the three models and is associated with small increases (.6%) in homicide rates even when the conviction gap is considered. The coefficient representing the disadvantage index is .25867 in the conviction gap model suggesting that as the disadvantage scale increases by one unit, rates of homicide increase by nearly thirty percent. The coefficient for Southern region (.35802) is also in the predicted direction. The relationship between Southern region and homicide rates is significant at the .01 level, and states located in the South have murder rates that are, on average, forty-three percent higher than non-Southern states. Percentage of young males in the population is the only sociodemographic variable in the model that fails to significantly predict general homicide rates.

The period variables in Model 2 have negative coefficients. However, similar to the results in Model 1, only time period 2 (1996-2000) is significant. State homicide rates were 31.1 percent lower in 1996-2000 than they were in 1991-1996. Time 3 (2001- 2004), however, is not significantly associated with homicide rates.

Time from Sentence to Execution. Continuing the pattern from the previous two models, Model 3 from Table 5.1 illustrates that the deterrence variables in the model are not significant predictors of homicide rates. Specifically, the coefficient representing the wait from sentence to execution is -.00062, but again, this effect is insignificant. The celerity dummy variable, time alive on death row variable, and the time alive on death row dummy variable are not significant in Model 3.

Model 3 in Table 5.1 also shows that most of the sociodemographic variables significantly predict homicide rates. The relationship between percent metropolitan and homicide rates is significant at the .01 level and is in the predicted direction. The results indicate that a percentage increase in metropolitan population is associated with a .6 percent increase in the homicide rates. The effect of disadvantage in Model 3 is significant at the .001 level and shows that as levels of disadvantage increase, rates of homicide also increase by thirty percent. Consistent with the effect of young males in Models 1 and 2, this variable fails to predict homicide rates in Model 3. The result for Southern region is significant at the .01 level and is in the predicted direction. Southern states have murder rates that are forty-two percent higher than their non-Southern counterparts.

The period variables in Model 3 in Table 5.1 are both negative, however, only the time period 2 (1996-2000) variable is significantly related to reductions in state homicide rates. The coefficient of -.36006 suggests that homicide rates in time 2 (1996-2000) are on average thirty percent lower than rates in time period 1 (1991-1995).

Summary of Models Assessing the Role of Celerity of Executions on State Homicides

Overall, the findings suggest that regardless of how expediently executions are carried out, or which measure of celerity is considered, waits on death row, fail to significantly reduce homicides. As the models in Table 5.1 illustrate, the celerity measures are not significantly related to state homicide rates. Disadvantage, percent metropolitan, southern region and the period from 1996-2000, are, however, significantly associated with homicides. In fact, the offense, conviction, and sentencing gaps, as well as the other deterrence variables are insignificant across the three models. Instead, the most consistent predictors of homicide rates are disadvantage, and the time period from 1996-2000. For example, a one unit increase in disadvantage is associated with about a thirty percent increase in state homicide rates. In addition, compared to time 1 (1991-1995), time 2 (1996-2000) had over thirty percent fewer homicides.

Metropolitan areas also have significantly higher rates of homicide, albeit small. A one percentage increase in the percent of the state living in a metropolitan area is associated with less than a one percent (.602%) increase in the homicide rate, and this effect is similar across the models. Southern region is also strongly associated with increased homicide rates. Specifically, compared to non-Southern states, Southern states have an average of approximately forty-two percent more homicides.

Despite these insignificant effects for homicides among the general population, disaggregating the analysis by race may reveal a different pattern. In the next chapter, I explore this possibility by using race-specific celerity measures and race-specific homicide rates. The goal is to assess whether race plays a role in producing or inhibiting deterrence, regarding celerity in executions.

Chapter 6

Does Race Matter? Assessing the "Reach of Executions"

Perhaps the negligible findings for celerity in executions are due to the fact that the executions and homicides are not disaggregated by race. Doing so may uncover deterrent effects that may otherwise go unnoticed. To date, there have not been studies on celerity that disaggregate executions by race. Although Shepherd's (2004) study disaggregated homicides by race while assessing the role celerity has for deterring murders, her study does not indicate whether the race of the offender matters for deterrence to occur. Shepherd's analysis indicated that celerity in executions deters homicides of both blacks and whites. However, her study is the only one, thus far, on celerity to find empirical support for the deterrence hypothesis. Thus, it stands alone in the literature, and additional evidence is needed to help build our cumulative understanding of the role that race may have in producing or inhibiting deterrence.

Currently, we have limited evidence regarding whether blacks and whites are equally affected by how quickly executions are carried out, and we do not know whether the role of celerity in executions varies with the race of the executed. Although Classical School arguments assume that individuals weigh equally the costs and rewards of punishment, this may be a faulty assumption. Different groups have different experiences with punishment and the justice system. As such, they may weigh the costs of punishment versus the rewards of killing differently. In the United States, this is particularly true of different racial and ethnic groups as discussed in Chapter 2.

Previously (Chapter 2), I provided arguments for why race may matter for deterrence. Drawing on empirical work from the racial identity, communication, and perceptions of injustice literatures, I argue that members of racial groups are more likely to form alliances with and identify with individuals who are similar in race to themselves. As such, the execution of a member of one racial group may not be able to deter members of another group because deterrence is a communication process that relies on the deterrent message being successfully delivered. In the case of celerity in executions, in order for deterrence to occur, would-be murderers must be able to see themselves receiving the same punishment for committing an offense similar to the offense committed by the executionee. This raises questions about whether black and white populations can be deterred by the execution of someone who is of a different race.

Prior research has shown that in the United States, blacks are more likely to believe that the criminal justice system treats their racial group more harshly than other racial groups (Bobo and Johnson 2004; Brunson 2007) , and whites are more likely than other groups to believe that the system is fair and neutral. Given that race continues to be a salient factor in U.S. society, whites may view themselves as being so different from blacks in terms of crime and justice that it becomes difficult for whites to place themselves in the shoes of a black person being executed for a capital offense. As a result, whites may not be able to be deterred by celerity in the execution of blacks. This is not surprising because, historically whites, the dominant racial group, made great efforts to distinguish themselves from blacks through the implementation of Jim Crow laws, residential segregation, and the one-drop rule (Thernstrom 2000). Blacks, however, may be deterred by the execution of whites since they are more likely to view themselves as being treated more harshly than whites by the criminal justice system. Thus, at the very least when whites are executed, it may signal to blacks that they can expect to be treated as harshly as white executionees for committing a capital murder.

Race-Specific Results

In light of the non-significant findings for the deterrence measures considered in the general models and the correlations among the celerity measures (see Table 4.6), the race-specific analyses will utilize just one of the celerity measures: time from sentence to execution. The choice of sentence celerity is somewhat arbitrary but reflects the point of celerity that is involved in contemporary discussions of court challenges. From a strictly Classical School point of view, it is the time elapsed between the offense and the punishment that is important for deterrence. However it is possible that the conviction or the sentence may symbolize the point at which official accountability for a capital offense may begin. After running all of the models using the three different measures and finding similar results, I use the sentence gap in all forthcoming models for several reasons.

First, it is the time that elapses between the sentence and the execution that has been the focus of policy debates surrounding time spent on death row. Long waits for the administration of executions after a death sentence raise questions about whether death row inmates are receiving cruel and unusual punishment. It has been argued that the additional punishment of living in solitary confinement for several years prior to the administration of the death sentence may violate the Eighth Amendment (Time on Death Row 2005). Solitary confinement is considered a severe form of punishment for prisoners in the general population that can only be used for short periods of time. Inmates on death row, however, live in solitary confinement for extended periods of time and the isolation often results in the deterioration of their mental health (Smith, 2008). While such waits can be viewed as the consequence of convicted offenders filing appeals, lawmakers have yet to find a way to allow offenders to exercise their rights to file appeals while ensuring that prisoners are not inflicted with cruel and unusual punishment, on account of excessive waits on death row (Time on Death Row, 2005).

Second, after an offense or a conviction, there is still the possibility of receiving other sentences besides the death penalty. Thus, any period before a formal sentence to death is typically not time spent on death row awaiting an execution. As such, only those with a formal sentence to death are even eligible to be housed on death row. Thus, although many capital offenders who are sentenced to death never actually serve time on death row, from this view, the sentence gap is the most precise measurement of how long offenders wait to be executed.

Third, the offense, conviction, and sentence gaps are highly correlated (see Table 4.6) indicating that they are measuring overlapping concepts. For example, the offense gap is correlated at .959 with the conviction gap. Similarly, the conviction gap is correlated with the sentence gap at .901. With such high correlations among the celerity measures, it is not surprising that I obtained similar results using the three different measures.

Finally, the gap between sentencing and execution has thus far been the only measure used in both previous studies of celerity. For comparative purposes, I also seek to keep in line with the tradition of prior studies examining the role of celerity. Therefore, all models henceforth measure celerity with the sentencing gap. I begin by presenting a descriptive picture of the measures in the analyses.

Descriptive Results

Homicides. Table 6.1 presents the descriptive statistics of the race-specific variables. The average homicide counts vary little by race. Discussion of these data is supplemented by figures from more detailed descriptive information that are not shown. In death penalty states from 1991-2004 there was an average of 160 white homicide offenders per state-year group period compared to 158 black homicide offenders. The number of white offenders ranged from a low of six (Delaware) to a high of 1,887 (California). Several states (e.g. Idaho, Montana, New Hampshire, South Dakota, and Wyoming) did not have any black homicide offenders during at least one of the state-year group periods (see Table 6.2) although the number of black homicides reached as high as 818.[15]

Celerity of White and Black Executions. Table 6.1 shows the mean number of months whites and blacks waited after sentencing before their execution. Whites waited an average of 120.87 months while blacks waited 149.68 months, over two years longer than whites. White waits from sentencing to execution ranged from fourteen to 242 months and black waits ranged from sixty-four to 275 months.

Executions. On average, there were about seven executions per state-year group (see Table 4.1 in Chapter 4), with whites accounting for about 4.5 and blacks accounting for 2.7 executions. Texas (not shown) had the most executions among blacks (43) and whites (91). In addition, Idaho, Kentucky, Mississippi, Montana, Nevada, New Mexico, Oregon, Pennsylvania, and Tennessee, executed only white offenders and did not execute any black offenders during the entire study period (not shown).

Disadvantage. Whites and blacks differ on levels of disadvantage as well as the variables that are included in the disadvantage index. For example, Table 6.1 shows that the average percentage of whites living in female-headed households is 7.67 percent. However, the rate for blacks living in female-headed households is 25.20 percent, over three times higher compared to whites. A closer look at the distribution indicates that although the ranges vary tremendously, overall both whites and blacks had the lowest percentage of female-headed households in South

---

[15] There were not any black homicide offenders in Idaho from 1991-1995, Montana from 1991-2000, New Hampshire from 1991-2000, South Dakota from 1991-1995 and 2001-2004, and Wyoming from 1996-2000.

Table 6.1. Descriptive Statistics for Race-Specific Dependent, Deterrence and Sociodemographic Variables

VARIABLE NAME	MEAN	STANDARD DEVIATION	MINI.	MAXI.
Dependent Variables				
White Homicide Offenders	160.13	263.86	6.00	1887.00
Black Homicide Offenders	158.78	169.56	0.00	818.00
Deterrence Variables				
White Celerity (months)	120.87	70.96	14.00	242.00
Black Celerity (months)	149.68	77.15	64.00	275.00
White Executions	4.54	11.72	0.00	91.00
Black Executions	2.68	7.33	0.00	43.00
Sociodemographic Variables				
White Disadvantage	0.01	0.78	-1.59	2.62
White Female-Headed Households	7.67	0.76	6.05	9.69
White Poverty	9.72	2.64	4.64	18.03
White Unemployment	3.10	0.53	2.06	4.40
Black Disadvantage	-0.01	0.84	-2.31	2.42
Black Female-Headed Households	25.20	6.75	4.95	34.03
Black Poverty	26.05	6.49	12.57	46.42
Black Unemployment	7.03	1.15	3.58	10.43
Young White Males	14.14	0.98	11.54	16.98
Young Black Males	17.38	3.54	13.93	27.99
White Population	4,487,584	4,292,556	427,220	20,555,653
Black Population	767,458	790,159	2,047	2,962,862

N: 111

Dakota (not shown). Among whites, the percentage of female-headed households ranged from a low of six percent (South Dakota) to a high of almost ten percent (Kentucky). Blacks however, had higher percentages of female-headed households, ranging from nearly five percent (South Dakota) up to thirty-four percent in (Illinois) during the 1991-1995 period.

The percentage of the population living in poverty also varies by race. The data indicate that on average, blacks are well over twice as likely to live in poverty compared to their white counterparts. White poverty ranged from less than five percent to eighteen percent. Conversely, black poverty ranged from about thirteen percent; well over twice the rate of the lowest level of poverty for whites, to a high of forty-six percent.

The percent unemployed is also a component of the disadvantage index that varies among blacks and whites. As shown in Table 6.1, on average, blacks have an unemployment rate that is twice that of whites. Among blacks, the unemployment rate reached a high of 10.43 percent although the highest it reached for whites was only 4.40. The lowest rates of unemployment were 2.1 percent for whites and 3.6 percent for blacks.

Young Males. The data indicate that there are higher percentages of young black males (17.36%) in death penalty states compared to young white males (14.10%). A closer look at the data reveals that the state with the highest percentage of young black males is South Dakota (not shown). Almost twenty-eight percent of South Dakota's black population was comprised of young males. Virginia (not shown) had the highest percentage of young white males who made up slightly less than seventeen percent of the white population.

Racial Differences in State Homicide Rates

Table 6.2 presents the 1995, 2000, and 2004 white and black homicide rates by regions. As shown, black homicide rates are on average 6.6 times higher than white homicide rates and this pattern is consistent across regions. In fact, only Nebraska in 2000 had white homicide rates that were higher than the black homicide rate for the same period. In 1995, the average homicide rate was 3.87 for whites and 27.90 for blacks. This gap narrowed slightly in 2000 when the homicide rate for both racial groups declined to 2.95 for whites and 16.50 for blacks. By 2004, homicide rates for both whites and blacks had increased; the rate rose to 3.47 for whites compared to 24.07 for blacks.

In 1995, whites had the highest homicide rate in Arizona (11.19) while blacks had the highest homicide rate in Nevada (61.29). The lowest homicide rates were in Nebraska during this period for both whites (.88) and blacks (1.75). In 2000, white homicide rates peaked to 9.84 in New Mexico followed by Arizona (7.55). However, black homicide rates soared well above the rates for whites with the highest homicide rates for blacks reaching over thirty in Pennsylvania. In 2000, whites had the lowest homicide rate in Kentucky (.61) while blacks continued to experience their lowest homicide rate in Nebraska (1.81). In 2004, Arizona once again had the highest homicide rates for whites (8.68) while blacks experienced their highest homicide rates in Idaho (41.54). Overall, average homicide rates were highest in the West for both whites (5.14) and blacks (31.05) and lowest in the Midwest for whites (1.77) and in the Northeast for blacks (16.61).

Table 6.2: Race Specific State Homicide Rates in 1995, 2000, and 2004 for Whites and Blacks

State	1995		2000		2004	
	White	Black	White	Black	White	Black
Northeast						
Connecticut	1.92	23.40	2.12	12.63	1.18	10.24
New Hampshire	1.20	0	1.19	0	0.85	12.06
New Jersey	2.10	18.16	1.67	12.35	2.59	14.74
New York	2.77	17.02	2.47	13.79	1.98	11.10
Pennsylvania	1.95	42.39	1.63	30.49	2.01	30.74
Midwest						
Illinois	2.21	32.53	0.95	12.20	1.08	13.66
Indiana	2.19	30.48	1.63	22.37	1.51	27.56
Kansas	-	-	1.83	3.38	2.60	17.56
Missouri	2.72	51.39	1.62	29.27	2.71	27.16
Nebraska	0.88	1.75	1.81	1.51	1.60	3.01
Ohio	1.50	26.82	1.41	11.34	1.63	16.73
South						
Alabama	2.66	21.77	1.66	11.15	2.01	10.98
Arkansas	4.58	43.65	3.00	23.80	2.38	20.67
Delaware	1.12	2.68	2.64	11.55	1.06	4.08
Florida	3.41	20.79	-	-	-	-
Georgia	3.50	23.38	2.38	10.57	2.71	11.09
Kentucky	4.16	21.75	0.61	9.94	3.79	14.40
Louisiana	2.99	32.57	3.04	24.22	2.68	28.11
Maryland	2.74	29.77	2.59	17.15	2.62	17.15
Mississippi	1.71	15.18	2.49	12.44	1.79	12.54
North Carolina	4.23	27.55	3.38	20.75	2.66	17.03
Oklahoma	7.65	40.04	4.81	24.23	5.44	22.27
South Dakota	1.41	0	1.20	22.31	1.65	0
Tennessee	3.43	34.49	3.30	26.03	3.57	24.63
Texas	8.16	29.08	7.27	16.56	7.12	18.17
Virginia	3.13	24.59	2.86	20.49	2.58	18.38
West						
Arizona	11.19	49.06	7.55	15.73	8.68	29.42
California	9.18	37.20	7.28	20.81	7.86	23.60
Colorado	5.53	33.53	2.84	23.39	5.03	33.13
Idaho	5.99	0	1.41	20.77	4.04	41.54
Montana	2.56	0	0.99	0	3.71	181.74
Nevada	7.50	61.29	5.07	18.56	6.53	21.66
New Mexico	8.01	16.77	9.84	13.51	14.02	33.77
Oregon	4.32	52.84	1.96	25.51	3.19	17.66

Note: - denotes missing data.

Table 6.2: Race Specific State Homicide Rates in 1995, 2000, and 2004 for Whites and Blacks (Continued)

State	1991-1995		1996-2000		2001-2004	
	White	**Black**	**White**	**Black**	**White**	**Black**
South Carolina	4.11	28.65	4.67	24.22	4.63	22.01
Utah	4.82	45.13	1.94	27.00	3.25	27.00
Washington	4.31	35.97	3.27	20.56	3.25	21.68
Wyoming	1.40	60.79	2.74	0	2.28	33.27
Mean	**3.87**	**27.9**	**2.95**	**16.5**	**3.47**	**24.07**

Racial Differences in Waits for Executions

Table 6.3 presents racial differences in the celerity of executions based on the sentence to execution gap by state and year groups. As shown in this table whites are being executed more swiftly than blacks and this pattern is consistent across the three periods. For executions during the 1991-1995 period, on average, blacks had waited an average of 28.89 months (2.41 years) longer to be executed than whites (i.e., 115 months versus 144 months for whites and blacks respectively). This difference in celerity by race was even larger during the 1996-2000 period with blacks waiting 32.74 months (2.73 years) longer than whites on death row. By 2001-2004, this gap was narrowing and blacks were waiting an average of 147.59 months (12.30 years) compared to 122.81 months (10.23 years) for whites.

Table 6.3 also shows that Pennsylvania was the only northeastern state to execute, and only whites were executed in Pennsylvania during the study period. Thus, there were not any black executions in the northeast from 1991-2004. The Midwestern states allow for a better comparison of celerity in executions among whites and blacks. Among the Midwest state-year groups with both black and white executions, blacks waited longer than whites

Table 6.3. Mean Sentence Gaps by State, Race and Year Groups

State	1995		2000		2004	
	White	Black	White	Black	White	Black
Northeast (137)						
Connecticut	-	-	-	-	-	-
New Hampshire	-	-	-	-	-	-
New Jersey	-	-	-	-	-	-
New York	-	-	-	-	-	-
Pennsylvania	142.00	-	132.00	-	-	-
Midwest (155.27)						
Illinois	176.25	181.50	117.00	197.00	-	-
Indiana	149.00	161.00	104.50	190.50	139.25	-
Kansas	-	-	-	-	-	-
Missouri	122.80	115.14	125.06	137.55	134.00	155.75
Nebraska	-	195.00	141.00	234.00	-	-
Ohio	-	-	102.00	-	180.78	201.60
South (128.59)						
Alabama	108.00	152.00	165.75	195.57	174.71	-
Arkansas	108.33	64.00	105.50	107.50	26.00	130.50
Delaware	14.00	118.00	91.67	119.33	154.00	101.00
Florida	141.25	156.33	-	-	-	-
Georgia	133.25	103.00	96.33	-	213.58	275.00
Kentucky	-	-	196.50	-	-	-
Louisiana	149.00	104.50	142.00	143.67	114.00	-
Maryland	26.00	-	-	120.50	158.00	-
Mississippi	-	-	-	-	166.00	-
North Carolina	119.20	-	110.80	140.33	107.50	124.57
Oklahoma	123.25	161.00	136.75	167.50	153.34	126.27
South Carolina	102.00	185.00	151.55	175.44	113.00	166.00
Tennessee	-	-	227.00	-	-	-
Texas	117.03	135.31	135.78	146.53	122.31	118.17
Virginia	81.13	119.20	84.14	81.25	46.82	77.00
West (117)						
Arizona	125.75	-	184.82	-	-	-
California	136.00	-	192.25	202.00	165.50	-
Colorado	-	-	123.00	-	-	-
Idaho	21.00	-	-	-	-	-
Montana	242.00	-	109.00	-	-	-
Nevada	-	61.29	82.00	-	65.67	-
New Mexico	-	16.77	-	-	65.00	-
Oregon	-	52.84	42.00	-	-	-

Note: Mean number of months by region is in parentheses.

Table 6.3. Mean Sentence Gaps by State, Race and Year Groups (Continued)

State	1991-1995		1996-2000		2001-2004	
	White	Black	White	Black	White	Black
South Dakota	-	-	-	-	-	-
Utah	-	212.00	106.50	-	-	-
Washington	83.50	-	32.00	-	34.00	-
Wyoming	116.00	-	-	-	-	-
Mean Month	**115.31**	**144.20**	**124.50**	**157.24**	**122.81**	**147.59**
Total Executions	**102**	**65**	**234**	**127**	**184**	**74**

on death row with the exception of Missouri from 1991-1995 where whites waited an average of 122.80 months (10.23 years) compared to only 115.14 months (9.6 years) for blacks. States located in the Southern region are most likely to execute both blacks and whites. In fact, among the Southern states, Arkansas, Delaware, Oklahoma, South Carolina, Texas and Virginia executed both blacks and whites during each period.

Overall, as illustrated in Table 6.3, blacks in every region spend a greater number of months waiting to be executed compared to whites. This difference in greatest in the West where blacks waited an average of 100 months (8.33 years) longer than whites for executions. This in part, could be due to the fact that the only western jurisdictions that executed both blacks and whites were California and Utah and these states followed the familiar pattern of taking longer to execute blacks than whites after sentencing. The smallest difference in waits from sentence to execution among whites and blacks is in the South. In southern states whites are executed an average of 13.58 months (1.3 years) sooner than blacks.

Of the few state-year groups that execute blacks more celeritously, all of them are located in the South. These states include, Arkansas, Georgia, and Louisiana during the 1991-1995 period, Virginia from 1996-2000, and Delaware, Oklahoma, and Texas from 2001-2004.

Are Whites and Blacks Differentially Deterred?

Table 6.4 presents the results from the negative binomial regression models with homicides disaggregated by race. I assess if whites and blacks are differentially deterred by celerity in general executions. I find that, the gap in months from sentences to executions for all executionees is insignificant for both whites (-.00085) and blacks (-.00211). Contrary to propositions offered by deterrence theory, the swiftness with which executions occur has no appreciable impact on either white or black homicide rates, and these results are consistent with the aggregated results presented in Chapter 5. The celerity dummy coefficient (-.45047) however, is statistically significant for blacks and the average time alive on death row dummy coefficient (-.56196) is significant for whites. The coefficients indicate that black homicide rates are forty-three percent lower in state-year groups without executions, and white homicide rates are nearly thirty-six percent lower in state-year groups that did not have any individuals waiting on death row.[16] This suggests that the death penalty

---

[16] The unit change is calculated by subtracting e^b from one and then multiplying it by 100 (Long 1997: 225). Using the example of the sentence gap from Table 5.1, the unit change is calculated as $(e^{-.001}-1)*100 = .10$. Using this formula allows for a more straightforward interpretation of the negative binomial regression coefficients. Essentially, this indicates a percentage change in the outcome (homicides) for every one unit change in the explanatory variable.

Table 6.4. Negative Binomial Regression Analysis of the Effect of Celerity in General Executions on White and Black Homicide Rates

	WHITES	BLACKS
DETERRENCE VARIABLES		
Sentence Celerity (All races combined)	-.00085	-.00211
	(.00115)	(.00123)
Sentence Celerity Dummy	-.18680	-.45047*
	(.16690)	(.22569)
Avg. Time Alive on Death Row	-.00104	.00271
	(.00203)	(.00158)
Avg. Time Alive on Death Row Dummy	-.56196*	-.13163
	(.24568)	(.23723)
Certainty (All executions combined)	.00208	.00142
	(.00263)	(.00246)
SOCIODEMOGRAPHIC VARIABLES		
Metropolitan	.00549*	.00280
	(.00260)	(.00552)
Disadvantage	.42593***	.11934
	(.10584)	(.08819)
Young Males	.12187*	.03142
	(.05896)	(.03251)
Southern Region	.08470	-.09112
	(.14237)	(.18369)
TIME PERIOD		
Time 2 (1996-2000)	-.06870	-.46532***
	(.12249)	(.09525)
Time 3 (2001-2004)	.33859	-.41062**
	(.17836)	(.15271)
CONSTANT	-12.39578***	-8.78937***
	(.94289)	(.93771)
Wald χ^2 (11df)	123.75	102.98

Note: Standard Errors are in parentheses. *p<.05, **p<.01, ***p<.001 (one-tailed).

may have a brutalizing effect (see Chapter 2) on both whites and blacks (Bowers and Pierce, 1980) because the findings suggest that homicide rates may be reduced for blacks if there are no executions and reduced for whites if nobody is on death row.

The sociodemographic variables in the models are significantly associated with only white state homicide rates. Percent metropolitan, percent disadvantage, and percent young males are, as hypothesized, positively associated with white homicide rates. These socio-demographic variables, however, fail to predict black homicide rates. Disadvantage significantly predicts white homicide rates. Based on the results, a one unit increase in disadvantage is associated with a fifty-three percent increase in white homicide offenders. Percent metropolitan also has a positive effect on white homicide rates such that a one percentage increase in the proportion of the state living in a metropolitan area is associated with a .5 percent increase in homicides. Another factor significantly impacting white homicide rates is the percentage of young white males living in the state. Every percentage increase in young white males is associated with an increase of nearly thirteen percent more white homicide offenders. Southern region is insignificant in both the white and black models. The coefficients for Southern region (.08470) indicate that the homicide rates of blacks and whites in the South are not significantly different from black and white homicides rates in non-Southern states. The period variables are only significant in the model predicting black homicides. This suggests that white homicide rates from neither 1996-2000 nor 2001-2004 are significantly different from homicide rates during 1991-1995. The black homicide rate, however, decreased significantly during both comparison periods.

Compared to the period 1991-1995 there were thirty-seven percent fewer black homicides from 1996-2000 and nearly thirty-four percent fewer homicides from 2001-2004.

Overall, the models in Table 6.4 suggest that neither blacks nor whites are deterred by the length of time the general population of death sentenced offenders spend waiting for their executions. However, not having individuals executed is shown to reduce black homicide rates and not having offenders on death row is shown to reduce white homicide rates. Moreover, white and black homicide rates are influenced by different variables. While, the sociodemographic factors are significant predictors of white homicides, they have no meaningful impact on black homicide rates. Instead, black homicide rates are predicted by the period variables, which indicate that compared to the period 1991-1995, black homicide rates declined during 1996-2000 as well as 2001-2004.

Does the Race of the Executed Offender Matter for Deterrence?

To delve into the relationship between race and deterrence further, I also present models that assess whether the race of the executed matters for reducing state homicide rates. Table 6.5 presents the results of racially disaggregated homicides as well as executions. Specifically, I assess whether celerity in white executions impact white homicide rates and whether celerity in black executions impact black homicide rates controlling for race-specific sociodemographic conditions. The findings indicate, that the number of months whites and blacks wait to be executed is inconsequential for reducing their respective racial groups' homicide rates.

The celerity dummy variable is significant for blacks and the average time alive on death row dummy is significant for whites. States that do not have black executions have a twenty-three percent lower black homicide rate and states that do not have anyone waiting on death row have a forty-four percent lower white homicide rate. Thus, although how long someone waits to be executed may not be consequential for white or black homicide rates, whether someone is executed is consequential for black homicide rates and whether someone is on death row is consequential for white homicide rates. This is true even in the race-specific models where executions and homicides are disaggregated by race. Similar to the general results in Chapter 5, these findings contradict the deterrence theory hypothesis related to celerity of executions.

With regard to the sociodemographic variables, Table 6.5 shows that while they explain white homicide rates, they fail to significantly predict black homicide rates. With the exception of Southern region, all of the sociodemographic control variables are significant in the white model although none of them are significant for blacks. States that have more white individuals living in metropolitan areas, higher levels of disadvantage among whites, and a higher percentage of young white males have significantly higher homicide rates among whites. The coefficient for metropolitan is .00543 representing a .50 percent increase for every percentage increase in percent metropolitan. The disadvantage coefficient (.42925) suggests that for every unit increase in white disadvantage, the white homicide rate increases by fifty-three percent.

Table 6.5. Negative Binomial Regression Analysis Comparing the Effect of Celerity of White and Black Executions on Race-specific State Homicide Rates

	WHITES	BLACKS
DETERRENCE VARIABLES (Race-specific)		
Sentence Celerity (Race-specific)	-.00039	-.00096
	(.00097)	(.00080)
Sentence Celerity Dummy	-.12138	-.26710*
	(.13632)	(.12450)
Avg. Time Alive on Death Row	-.00122	.00195
	(.00200)	(.00171)
Avg. Time Alive on Death Row Dummy	-.57286**	-.18151
	(.24335)	(.22998)
Certainty (Race-Specific Executions)	.00427	.00425
	(.00480)	(.00579)
SOCIODEMOGRAPHIC VARIABLES		
Metropolitan	.00543**	.00247
	(.00258)	(.00550)
Disadvantage (Race-specific)	.42925***	.12219
	(.10333)	(.09666)
Young Males (Race-specific)	.11968**	.03028
	(.05809)	(.03248)
Southern Region	.08547	-.06482
	(.14124)	(.18435)
TIME PERIOD		
Time 2 (1996-2000)	-.07162	-.47800***
	(.11911)	(.09359)
Time 3 (2001-2004)	.34260	-.40429**
	(.17610)	(.15176)
CONSTANT	-12.41378***	-8.873***
	(.94166)	(.93595)
Wald χ^2 (11df)	127.50	117.62

N=111

Note: Standard Errors are in parentheses. *p<.05, **p<.01, ***p<.001 (one-tailed).

In addition, the coefficient for percent young males is .11968 and represents a twelve percent increase in the white homicide rate for every one percentage increase of young white males.

Finally, the period variables are only significant for the black homicide rate. Compared to the homicide rate during time period 1 (1991-1995), homicide rates are nearly thirty-eight percent lower for blacks during time period 2 (1996-2000) and thirty-three percent lower during time period 3 (2001-2004).

Does Celerity in the Execution of Whites Affect Black Homicide Rates?

Table 6.6 presents the results from the model examining whether celerity in white executions serves to deter black homicides. The simple answer to whether white executions deter blacks is no. Rather, contrary to deterrence theory, longer waits on death row among whites is negatively associated with black state homicide rates, although this association is insignificant. In fact, all of the deterrence measures in Table 6.6 fail to significantly influence black homicide rates.

The sociodemographic variables in Table 6.6 also fail to significantly explain black homicide rates, thus, black sociodemographic conditions do not influence the occurrence of murder for blacks. The time period variables are the only variables in the model that significantly explain black homicide rates. The coefficient for time period 2 is -.48265 and the coefficient for time period 3 is -.40259 which indicates that from 1996-2000 states had black homicide rates that were thirty-eight percent lower than the rate from 1991-1995, and from 2001-2004 rates were thirty-three percent lower than for the comparison

Table 6.6. Negative Binomial Regression Analysis of Celerity of White Executions on Black Homicide Rates

	BLACKS
DETERRENCE VARIABLES	
Sentence Celerity (Whites only)	-.00004
	(.00099)
Celerity Dummy	-.20519
	(.18140)
Avg. Time Alive on Death Row	.00187
	(.00183)
Avg. Time Alive on Death Row Dummy	-.17906
	(.23004)
Certainty (White executions only)	.00167
	(.00363)
WHITE SOCIODEMOGRAPHIC VARIABLES	
Metropolitan	.00278
	(.00556)
Disadvantage (Blacks only)	.10563
	(.08686)
Young Males (Blacks only)	.03198
	(.03283)
Southern Region	-.07880
	(.18487)
TIME PERIOD	
Time 2 (1996-2000)	-.48265***
	(.08857)
Time 3 (2001-2004)	-.40259**
	(.15456)
CONSTANT	-8.97743***
	(1.00572)
Wald χ^2 (11df)	110.08

N=111

Note: Standard errors are in parentheses. *p<.05 one-tailed test; **p<.01 one-tailed test; ***p<.001 one-tailed test.

period. These results for the time period variables are similar to the findings presented for blacks in Tables 6.4 and 6.5.

Does Celerity in the Execution of Blacks Affect White Homicide Rates?

Table 6.7 presents the results testing whether celerity of black executions has any impact on whites to test whether racial identity matters for deterrence. The findings presented suggest that celerity in black executions fail to reduce white homicide rates. The celerity coefficient for black executions is -.00023 and has no measurable impact on white homicide rates. In addition, this coefficient is in the opposite direction of deterrence theory propositions. The average time on death row dummy variable, is significant and the coefficient (-.59389) represents a forty-five percent reduction in white homicides when there is no one on death row.

The sociodemographic variables, capturing white conditions, in Table 6.7 operate to influence white homicide rates, with the exception of Southern region. The coefficient for percent metropolitan is .00573 and corresponds to a .6 percent increase in homicides among whites for every one percent increase in percent metropolitan. Disadvantage (.44594) is significant at the p<.001 level and for every unit increase in disadvantage among whites, white homicides increase by fifty-six percent. The percentage of young white males in a state is also related to white homicide rates. The coefficient (.13222) presented in Table 6.7 suggests that for every percentage increase in young white males in the population, whites commit 14.14 percent more homicides.

Table 6.7. Negative Binomial Regression Analysis of Celerity of Black Executions on White Homicide Rates

	WHITES
BLACK DETERRENCE VARIABLES	
Sentence Celerity (Blacks only	-.00023
	(.00076)
Celerity Dummy	-.12100
	(.08864)
Avg. Time Alive on Death Row	-.00155
	(.00206)
Avg. Time Alive on Death Row Dummy	-.59389*
	(.24502)
Certainty (Black executions)	-.00138
	(.00556)
WHITE SOCIODEMOGRAPHIC VARIABLES	
Metropolitan	.00573*
	(.00271)
Disadvantage (Whites only)	.44594***
	(.10303)
Young Males (Whites only)	.13222*
	(.05728
Southern Region	.12505
	(.13531)
TIME PERIOD	
Time 2 (1996-2000)	-.03876
	(.12230)
Time 3 (2001-2004)	.39482*
	(.17765)
CONSTANT	12.620***
	(.91610)
Wald χ^2 (11df)	203.85

(N=111)

Note: Standard errors are in parentheses. *p<.05 one-tailed test; **p<.01 one-tailed test; ***p<.001 one-tailed test.

With regard to the time period variables, only time 3 is significantly related to white homicide rates. Specifically, compared to time 1 (1991-1995) homicide rates among whites were forty-eight percent higher during the 2001-2004 period.

Summary of Race-Specific Findings

Overall, the results indicate that celerity of executions fails to predict general and race-specific homicide rates. The sentence gap is consistently insignificant across the models illustrating that, irrespective of how long white and black offenders wait for their executions, homicide rates are not significantly impacted. Furthermore, in all of the models presented in this chapter, the celerity coefficients are negative, suggesting that longer waits are associated with decreases in homicides; a finding inconsistent with deterrence theory.

To answer the question of whether blacks and whites are differentially deterred by general executions, I present negative binomial regression models with homicides disaggregated by race. In these models, the effect of celerity is insignificant for whites
(-.00085) and blacks (-.00211), suggesting that neither blacks nor whites are deterred by waits in general executions. The celerity dummy and the average time on death row dummy variables have significant negative relationships but only impact either blacks or whites. On one hand, the celerity dummy variable has a significant negative impact on black homicide rates but fails to impact white homicide rates. This suggests that only black homicide rates are affected by whether someone is executed on death row; and the effect is inconsistent with deterrence theory. Compared to state-year groups when

people are executed, when people are not executed, state-year groups have thirty-six percent fewer black homicide offenders. On the other hand, the average time alive on death row dummy variable is only significantly affecting white homicide rates. State-years without anybody on death row are associated with over a forty percent reduction in white homicide rates; another finding contrary to deterrence theory. Put together, the effect of the celerity dummy variable on black homicides and the effect of the average time alive on death row dummy variable on white homicides suggest that eliminating executions and clearing death rows may be more effective for reducing homicide rates than speeding up executions. The other deterrence variables, namely certainty and average time alive on death row have no considerable impact on either white or black homicide rates.

Another important finding in this chapter is related to how the sociodemographic and time period variables operate differentially across the races. With the exception of the effect of southern region on black homicide rates, the sociodemographic variables operate in the predicted direction in both the white and black models. However, the sociodemographic variables are only consistently significantly impacting white homicide rates. For whites, metropolitan areas, higher levels of disadvantage, and a higher percentage of young males are associated with significant increases in homicide rates. These findings suggest that environmental factors help to explain white homicide rates. In fact, the sociodemographic variables do a better job of explaining white homicide rates than do the deterrence variables. Black homicide rates however, are consistently predicted by the time period variables in the models. Compared to time period 1 (1991-1995), time 2 black homicide rates decreased by thirty-seven percent and time period 3 had almost a thirty-four percent reduction.

In sum, the results indicate that race-specific homicide rates are predicted by different factors. The one similarity across the models is that neither black nor white homicide rates are significantly related to how quickly executions are carried out. Thus, neither whites nor blacks are deterred by celerity in executions, nor are there racial differences in their abilities to deter. In fact the sociodemographic variables and period variables are more consistent predictors of race-specific homicide rates than the deterrence variables. Overall, the results fail to support the deterrence hypothesis related to celerity. Moreover the coefficients are negative indicating that longer waits are actually associated with a reduction in homicides. Such findings lead me to conclude that shorter waits on death row are likely to fail miserably as an effective tool for deterring murders.

Chapter 7

Implications and Limitations of the Study

The findings presented in this study are consistent with the vast majority of previous studies examining the effect of capital punishment on deterrence. Utilizing negative binomial regression analysis, I find no support for the deterrence theory arguments regarding celerity of executions. Essentially, the speed at which executions occur has no implications for the occurrence of murder. Although some of the possible limitations of the study are identified in this final chapter, the results do not come as a surprise because they are consistent with a long line of death penalty research.

Waits on death row for executions after commission, conviction, and sentencing for a capital murder have become increasingly long. For example, in 1985 death row inmates spent nearly six years on death row prior to being executed but this wait had increased to over twelve years by 2005. Not surprisingly, these long waits have been a topic of debate. A part of this debate has centered on whether the death penalty can deter homicides if capital offenders wait, on average, over a decade for their executions. This study has addressed this question.

While research on the deterrent effects of severity, certainty, and publicity overwhelmingly fails to supports deterrence theory, there has been much less emphasis on the role of celerity, or the quickness, in which executions occur. The exceptions are studies by Bailey (1980) and Shepherd (2004) that yield inconsistent results. Bailey (1980) failed to find a significant effect of celerity for reducing homicide rates, while Shepherd's more recent study suggests that celerity is related to deterrence, with delays in executions undermining the deterrent value of the death penalty. Reconciling these contradictory findings was one of the goals of this research. Two additional goals were to determine whether the deterrent role of celerity is contingent on: (1) celerity being measured as the distance from the offense, conviction, or sentence to execution; (2) the race of executionees; or (3) the race of targeted audiences. Attention to the latter issues stems from the recognition in the racial identity and communication literatures that deterrence is a communication process that relies on threat messagesbeing conveyed to potential offenders. In order for would-be murderers to be deterred, they would need to envision themselves in the place of the person being executed. In a context such as the United States where different groups have very different experiences with, and views of, the criminal justice system and punishment, race may be an important contingency in whether one identifies with the executionee. However, work on deterrence theory has seldom assessed the "reach" of executions by examining whether racial groups have different responses to celerity of executions.

Thus far, only Shepherd's research has given attention to the impact race may have for deterrence by examining whether celerity in executions serves to reduce homicides for whites and blacks. Her study concludes that celerity in executions significantly reduces both white and black homicide rates. However, her study does not assess whether whites and blacks differentially produce deterrence. Given the continued importance of race in society, it is possible that audiences must be the same race as the offender in order for deterrence to occur. Finally, assessing the racial "reach" of the effect of celerity in executions on race-specific homicide rates addresses an assumption of deterrence theory that racial groups equally contemplate the costs and benefits of their actions, and thus, respond in the same manner to how quickly executions are carried out. Above, I have examined the scope of deterrence theory by testing whether the race of the audience and the executed need to be similar for deterrence to occur.

Understanding whether celerity contributes to deterrence may also be useful for policy makers given the implementation of *The Antiterrorism and Effective Death Penalty Act of 1996*, with its goal of shortening stays on death row. This legislation puts restrictions on the amount of time inmates on death row can file for appellate reviews. After being in place for over a decade, the time may be right to assess whether celerity matters for a variety of the presumed functions of capital punishment including deterrence.

Major Findings

In examining the above issues, I laid out a series of hypotheses related to how quickly executions occur. Hypothesis one proposed that shorter offense, conviction, and sentence gaps would be negatively related to state homicide rates and on the contrary, longer gaps would be positively related to state homicide rates. The analyses in

Chapter 5 (Table 5.1) shows that the three celerity gaps considered fail to significantly predict state homicide rates. This holds true when controlling for several sociodemographic predictors of homicide as well as time periods. Overall the models indicate that celerity in executions, irrespective of the measures considered, have no appreciable impact on state homicide rates. These findings are consistent with Bailey's (1980) prior work, contradictory to Shepherd's (2004) recent study, and fail to support the deterrence theory proposition regarding celerity.

I also hypothesized that greater celerity in general executions would be negatively related to both white and black homicide rates. Yet, the analyses in Chapter 6 fail to support this hypothesis. Interestingly, the celerity dummy variable, a dichotomous measure of state year-groups with and without executions is significantly related to black homicides. The negative direction of the coefficient (-.45047) indicates that there are thirty-six percent fewer black homicides in state-year groups that do not have executions. In addition, a dummy variable for the average time alive on death row predicts white homicide rates. On average, state-year groups without individuals waiting on death row experience about forty-three percent fewer white homicides. These race-specific findings are contrary to deterrence theory expectations.

This research also offered hypotheses related to whether the race of the executionee and the targeted audience must be similar for deterrence to occur. Consistent with the racial identity and communication literatures, I hypothesized that greater celerity in the execution of whites and blacks would have significant negative effects on their respective race-specific homicide rates. The results presented in Table 6.5 indicate that the race-specific celerity measures are not significantly related to the corresponding race-specific homicide rates.

Finally, this study delves further into the role of race for deterrence by examining whether white and black executions deter homicides for the other racial group. Drawing on arguments from research focusing on racial differences in perceptions of and experiences with the criminal justice system, I hypothesized that white executions would be able to deter black homicides, but black executions would not be significantly related to white homicide rates. I found that the celerity of white executions is not related to black homicide rates; nor does the swiftness of black executions affect white homicides. Indeed when only black executions are considered, the average time alive dummy variable is the only deterrence variable to significantly impact white homicide rates. The coefficient (-.59389) represents a forty-four percent decrease in white homicides in states without anyone waiting on death row. This finding contradicts deterrence theory as well.

In sum, the results show that the length of time offenders wait on death row is not related to state homicide rates. Moreover, race does not play a significant role for producing or inhibiting deterrence. Celerity in executions is unrelated to homicides when either general or race-specific measures of celerity are considered, and when homicides are disaggregated by race.

Theoretical Implications

The non-deterrence findings of this study are consistent with a long history of deterrence research. They provide no indication that shortening waits for executions has the theorized effect of reducing homicides rates. Importantly, these results remain consistent even when several different measures of celerity are considered. In fact, instead of findings consistent with deterrence, the analyses lend a bit of support to the brutalization argument (Bowers and Pierce 1980), which assumes that executions will be associated with higher rather than lower rates of homicide. The occurrence of executions (celerity dummy) and the presence of individuals waiting on death row (average time alive on death row dummy) are associated with higher homicide rates. This suggests that although celerity in executions as a dimension of punishment may not be relevant for reducing homicides, having someone on death row and executing even one offender may signal to the public that it is sometimes appropriate to kill. As a communication theory, deterrent messages sent by the use of capital punishment may be such that would-be offenders identify with the state as the executioner.

The race-specific findings also fail to support deterrence hypotheses. Not only does it not matter if executions are administered after long or short waits on death row, neither the race of the offender, nor the race of the targeted audience, is related to homicide rates. The racial identity arguments presented apparently do not apply to deterrence messages in the form of celerity of executions. While racial groups may be inclined to feel that they have more in common with people that share a similar ethnic background (Helms 1993; Newcomb 1961), as it relates to capital punishment, the messages associated with swifter executions may be too far removed for the vast majority of any racial group to envision an execution being their fate. Capital offenders are typically convicted of heinous crimes and most member of any population may be likely to view themselves as being too different from individuals capable of capital murder, even if they are similar in race. Thus, in terms of deterrence, both whites and blacks are seemingly unable to put themselves in the shoes of executed offenders irrespective of their race.

An alternative reason for the negligible findings related to celerity in executions may be that the deterrent effects of legal punishment are contingent upon each other. For example, Tittle (1969), argued that severity of punishment is only a deterrent when there is a high risk of certainty of punishment. Grasmick and Bryjak (1980) tested Tittle's (1969) arguments and illustrated that perceived certainty has a stronger effect when levels of perceived severity are high and that perceived severity has a stronger effect when levels of certainty are high. Albeit, neither Tittle (1969) nor Grasmick and Bryjak (1980) were examining the role of capital punishment as a deterrent, the same principles should apply. As it stands, only a small percentage of murder cases are actually sanctioned with a death sentence, and nearly half of these are reversed. Judge Noonan expressed a concern about this in his dissent in *Jeffers v. Lewis* when he argued that the death penalty is only ineffective as a deterrent because too few offenders are ever executed (Kozinski and Gallagher 1995). Therefore, capital punishment may not be certain enough for celerity to matter for killings. In the above analysis, I control for certainty with a count of executions, however, even the states that rely on the death penalty most frequently may have so few executions that no matter how expeditious they are carried out, homicides may not be influenced. In other words, perhaps the death penalty, as we currently administer it, has no deterrent value because there are too few executions, coupled with average waits of over a decade for the implementation of the penalty. This combination may lower the cost of committing murder because instead of expecting to experience a quick death they are likely to assume that they will live several years after their death sentence. In addition, certainty in executions may be perceived to be too low among potential murderers for them to worry about the quickness of which a potential execution would be carried out.

Policy Recommendations

The analyses provided illustrates that celerity of executions fail to produce deterrence. Nonetheless, there are policy implications of these non-deterrence findings. In the following discussion, I offer suggestions that I hope will help to inform future debates regarding death penalty policy.

Abandoning Efforts to Speed up Executions. This study reveals that the length of time offenders wait for their executions does not impact homicide rates. This suggests that legislative efforts to curtail death row waits such as *The Antiterrorism and Effective Death Penalty Act of 1996* will do little to stop the occurrence of murders. As such, efforts to shorten death row waits for the sake of increasing deterrence could be abandoned without losses in public safety. Policy makers who are weighing the importance of shortening waits on death row versus providing capital offenders with adequate lengths of time to prepare appeals should make ensuring that offenders are provided with adequate appellate rights a priority.

One of the reasons that the capital punishment process takes so long is because our legal system provides for systematic reviews before a death sentence can be carried out. For example, in the vast majority of states, post-trial proceedings begin with an appeal that challenges the death sentence. Eventually many cases end up in state supreme courts followed by federal courts of appeals (Gould 2008; Kozinski and Gallagher 1995; Tabak 2008). In addition, states currently have more than half of their death penalty cases pending appeals because states have been unable to find lawyers willing and able to take the cases (Hines 2001). In fact, the death penalty has been considered the one area of law where there are too few lawyers willing and able to handle the existing caseloads (Aarons 1998; Bright 1994; Bright and Keenan 1995). Despite efforts over many years, state and federal courts have been unable to obtain enough lawyers to speed up the capital punishment process (Gould 2008).

Ironically, two popular arguments offered on behalf of capital offenders related to waits on death row are being criticized for clashing with one another. Essentially, the first argument involves ensuring that capital offenders have adequate lengths of time to prepare their appeals. Legislation such as *The Antiterrorism and Effective Death Penalty Act of 1996* attempts to shorten death row waits by putting limits on the reasons appeals can be filed as well as the amount of time inmates have to file such appeals. Such legislation may inhibit some offenders from being able to prove their innocence. The second argument pertains to long waits on death row constituting cruel and unusual punishment because several years of confinement is an additional punishment beyond the sentence of death. Judge Noonan, argued that the aforementioned arguments are incongruous. Noonan insists that arguing that states should not execute offenders too fast because their rights may be violated, while simultaneously arguing that long waits on death row constitute cruel and unusual punishment, when delays are necessary to provide appellate rights seems to be at odds. Unfortunately, states often fail to provide the legal representation and resources offenders are entitled to in a timely manner, while advocates of capital punishment are simultaneously pushing for efforts to speed up executions. Given that there is no risk of higher rates of homicides in less celeritous state-years, efforts to speed up executions in the name of deterrence could be abandoned without costs in terms of increased killings.

Other than deterrence, the death penalty has additional goals including retribution and incapacitation and therefore there may be tradeoffs in these areas if capital punishment were abolished. However, it may be possible to accomplish these additional goals in other ways. For example, crimes can be scored as a gradient such that murder is classified as the most severe offense worthy of the most severe punishment. Perhaps life imprisonment without the possibility of parole (LWOP) could serve the same purpose as the death penalty while entirely eliminating the possibility of executing an innocent person. Moreover, LWOP is viewed by many to be more tolerable than the death penalty. Proponents of capital punishment object to LWOP on the basis that without the threat of the death penalty, "lifers" would have nothing to lose if they killed someone in prison (Bohm 2007). Available evidence, however, suggests that prisoners sentenced to LWOP were no greater threat to other prisoners or correctional staff than death-sentenced inmates or other murderers sentenced to a prison term (Sorenson and Wrinkle 1996). In fact, wardens and superintendents of correctional institutions have claimed that "lifers are generally among the best behaved prisoners and are most frequently employed as house servants because they are considered among the safest of prisoners (Bohm 2007).

Although research has shown that rates of murder among incarcerated inmates are low (Bohm 2007), accomplishing the goal of retribution, may be complex (Finckernauer 1988). It may be common for the family of murder victims to feel that an execution is warranted after experiencing such an emotional loss. As for punishing in kind (i.e., eye for an eye), no other crime is punished in this way (Bedau 2004). For example, the state does not rape rapist, or burn down the house of arsonist. As such, retaliation in the form of an eye for an eye should be intolerable aspirations for a government because it is not required for retribution. Moreover, the public currently accepts lengthy imprisonment terms for other serious offenses, and in abolitionist states lengthy sentences are used as a way to restore the social balance.

Moratorium on Executions and Clearing Death Rows. The findings presented in Chapter 6 (Table 6.4) suggest that a moratorium on executions and death row sentences may serve to reduce both white and black state homicide rates. State-year groups without executions have black homicide rates that are thirty percent lower than state-year groups with at least one execution. Given that celerity and certainty do not deter homicides, if the goal is to save lives perhaps efforts should be made to eliminate the legal provision for executions. Similarly, this study shows that not having individuals on death row is associated with significantly lower homicide rates for whites. According to the findings of this study, if states were to clear death rows, white homicide rates could be reduced by over forty percent. These substantial reductions in homicides associated with not executing offenders and not having individuals on death row is evidence that the use of capital punishment may cause more harm than it prevents. Ironically, one of the most important goals of the death penalty is to deter would-be murderers; however, the use of capital punishment has failed to accomplish this goal. After considering the extraordinary costs associated with capital cases, the absence of a deterrent effect, and the fact that using capital punishment is associated with higher homicide rates, it would make sense to do away with a punishment that, according to this study, is contributing to higher rates of homicides among whites and blacks.

Limitations and Suggestions for Future Research

Missing Homicide Data. Problems with missing data could have contributed to the non-deterrence findings. To measure homicide counts and calculate homicide rates, I relied on the data published by the Federal Bureau of Investigation (in its SHR). Unfortunately, the SHR has a considerable amount of missing homicide data. For example, Florida is one of the most active death penalty states, having executed sixty-nine capital offenders since it re-enacted capital punishment legislation in 1972. Yet, Florida only reported homicides to the UCR for no more than two months from 1997-1999 (Maltz and Weiss 2006). Not having complete homicide data from such an active execution state omits important data and introduces potential bias in estimating the deterrent effect of celerity of executions (Fagan 2006). Specifically, Fagan (2006) criticizes many previous studies for merely dropping missing data points because it fails to include states that are not normally distributed. Such an omission of data may have introduced selection bias thereby distorting the regression coefficients and the standard errors. Future, researchers investigating the deterrent value of the death penalty will need to find ways to address the missing homicide data problems. Perhaps, requesting data from state agencies rather than relying on FBI data may be a possible solution. Comparisons with vital statistics data could be done to ensure that state homicide figures are reliable.

Another limitation is that this study focuses only on general homicides despite the fact that most homicides do not constitute capital murder. It is possible that the effects of celerity can only be revealed if capital murders are distinguished from non-capital killings. Despite previous studies on publicity having considered felony homicides (a capital crime in almost all death penalty jurisdictions) and having failed to find a deterrent effect (Peterson and Bailey 1991), focusing on only death penalty eligible murders may be useful in future studies on celerity of executions.

Adequacy of Celerity Measures. Although the current findings are consistent with a long line of capital punishment and deterrence research, it still may be premature to close off discussions about the role that celerity may have for producing deterrence. As such, other measures of celerity should be considered. Despite measuring celerity of executions as the gaps between offense to execution, conviction to execution, and sentence to execution, the length of time prior to executions is not related to homicide rates. The negligible effects for the three celerity measures considered may be due to not considering the appropriate time lapse. Currently, the point at which punishment begins remains unclear as well as knowledge of what the public takes notice of in evaluating the swiftness of executions.

One problem with testing for an effect of celerity is identifying the point at which "punishment" begins. Perhaps audiences are more in tune to an arrest which may be considered the initial stage of punishment, although, the formal initiation (i.e., incarceration) of punishment may not begin for months or even years after a formal charge. The arrest is typically the gateway into the criminal justice system for offenders, and in many ways begins the process of being held accountable for a capital offense. Given the mound of evidence suggesting that executions are not related to homicide rates, it may be unlikely that the arrest gap will be related to homicides. However, examining whether the gap from arrests to executions is related to homicide rates may help researchers and policy makers to better speculate about the merits (or lack thereof) of the deterrence hypothesis for celerity of executions.

Examining Other Issues Impacted by Celerity of Executions. Celerity of executions may have other implications besides the ones offered by deterrence theory. How quickly executions are carried out may have implications for innocence, costs, discrimination, and the mental health of inmates on death row. Therefore, future researchers should consider addressing questions related to the potential impact of shortening death row waits. For example, among offenders who are found innocent, how long on average does it take for evidence that allows for such a conclusion to surface? Answering such questions could prove to be informative for policymakers in future debates about death row waits.

Other questions include whether making executions faster will affect some groups more than others? Would there be differences by gender, race of victims, or other factors? This research shows that whites are executed more celeritously than blacks. Such differences may imply that discrimination is taking place. It could be construed that discrimination is taking place against whites whose lives are taken more quickly, or against blacks because they are less likely to obtain legal counsel and therefore are more likely to suffer from mental illnesses such as death row syndrome. These complex research questions have not been answered and may have implications for future legislation on capital punishment.

Conclusion

This study has tested the effects of measures of celerity of executions on general and race-specific homicide rates controlling for important socio demographic variables and time periods. In doing so, I have investigated the deterrence theory hypothesis for celerity of executions. Essentially, my goal was to determine if jurisdictions that execute death row offenders more quickly have lower homicide rates than jurisdictions that take longer to execute, as hypothesized by deterrence theory. In addition, I assessed whether the race of executionees or targeted audiences matters for celeritous executions to produce deterrence. Based on the analyses, the simple answer to both questions is no; the length of time capital offenders wait before being executed is not statistically associated with homicide. This finding holds regardless of the celerity measure considered and regardless of whether homicides and/or executions are disaggregated by race. These results follow the pattern of a long history of capital punishment and deterrence research, which as a whole, refutes deterrence theory hypotheses. In fact, the results indicate that doing away with capital punishment would be beneficial for reducing both black and white homicide rates. Moreover, addressing sociodemographic challenges such as improving state levels of disadvantage may be more instrumental for reducing homicides than speeding up executions. Ironically, despite numerous studies illustrating that capital punishment having virtually no effect on crime, capital or otherwise, it continues to be favored by some including many aspiring politicians and some law enforcement officials. While the debate surrounding capital punishment is sure to continue, this study provides further evidence that the death penalty is not necessary to protect society from criminal killings.

References

Aarons, Dwight. 1998. "Getting Out of This Mess: Steps Toward Addressing and Avoiding Inordinate Delays in Capital Cases." *Journal of Criminal Law and Criminology* 89:1-80.

Agresti, Alan and Barabara Finlay. 1997. "Statistical Methods for the Social Sciences." Prentice Hall, Third Edition.

Allison, Paul. "Using Panel Data to Estimate the Effects of Events." *Sociological Methods and Research* 23:174-199.

Allison, Paul D. and Richard P. Waterman. 2002. "Fixed Effects Negative Binomial Regression Models." *Sociological Methodology* 32:247-265.

Almgren, Gunnar, Avery Guest, George Immerwahr, and Michael Spittel. 1998. "Joblessness, Family Disruption, and Violent Death in Chicago, 1970-1990." *Social Forces* 6(4):1465-1493.

Anderson, Elijah. 1999. *The Code of the Streets: Decency, Violence, and the Moral Life of the Inner City.* New York: Norton.

Baldus, David. C. and James W. L. Cole. 1975. "A Comparison of the Work of Thorsten Sellin and Isaac Ehrlich on the Deterrent Effect of Capital Punishment." *The Yale Law Journal* 85(2):170-186.

Bailey, William C. 1977. "Imprisonment vs. The Death Penalty as a Deterrent to Murder." *Law and Human Behavior* 1:239-260.

Bailey, William C. 1978. "Some Further Evidence on Imprisonment vs. the Death Penalty as a Deterrent to Murder." *Law and Human Behavior* 2(3):245-260.

Bailey, William C. 1980. "Deterrence and the Celerity of the Death Penalty: A Neglected Question in Deterrence Research." *Social Forces* 58(4):1308-1333.

Bailey, William C. 1982. "Capital Punishment and Lethal Assaults Against Police." *Criminology* 19:608-625.

Bailey, William C. 1983. "Disaggregation in Deterrence and Death Penalty Research: The Case of Murder in Chicago." *Journal of Criminal Law and Criminology* 74:827-59.

Bailey, William C. 1990. "Murder, Capital Punishment, and Television: Execution Publicity and Homicide Rates." *American Sociological Review* 55(5):628-633.

Bailey, William C. and Ruth D. Peterson. 1987. "Police Killings and Capital Punishment: The Post-Furman Period." *Criminology* 25:1-25.

Bailey, William C. and Ruth D. Peterson. 1989. "Murder and Capital Punishment: A Monthly Time-Series Analysis of Execution Publicity." *American Sociological Review* 54(5):772-43.

Bailey, William C. and Ruth D. Peterson. 1994. "Murder, Capital Punishment and Deterrence: A Review of the Evidence and an Examination of Police Killings." *Journal of Social Issues* 50(2):53-74.

Bashi, Vilna. 1998. "Racial Categories Matter because Racial Hierarchies Matter: A Commentary." *Ethnic and Racial Studies* 21:959-968.

Becker, Gary S. 1968. "Crime and Punishment: an Economic Approach." *Journal of Political Economy* 76: 169-217.

Bedau, Hugo Adam. 2004. "An Abolitionist's Survey of the Death Penalty in America Today," pp. 15-50 in Hugo Adam Bedau and Paul G. Cassell's *Debating the Death Penalty: Should America Have Capital Punishment? The Experts on Both Sides Make Their Best Case.* New York: Oxford.

Berk, Richard. 2005. "New Claims about Executions and General Deterrence: Déjà Vu All Over Again?" *Journal of Empirical Legal Studies* 2(2):303-330.

Blumstein, Alfred, Frederick P. Rivara, and Richard Rosenfeld. 2000. "The Rise and Decline of Homicide and Why." *Annual Review of Public Health* 21:505-541.

Blumstein, Alfred and Richard Rosenfeld. 2008. "Factors Contributing to U.S. Crime Trends" in *Understanding Crime Trends: Workshop Report.* The National Academy Press.

Bobo, Lawrence and Devon Johnson. 2004. "A Taste for Punishment: Black and white American's View on the Death Penalty and the War on Drugs. Du Bois Review 1:151-180.

Bohm, Robert M. *DeathQuest III: An Introduction to Theory and Practice of Capital Punishment in the United States,* Third Edition. Matthew Bender and Company, Inc.

Bonilla-Silva, Eduardo. 1999. "The Essential Social Factor of Race." *American Sociological Review* 64:899-906.

Bowers, William J. and Glenn L. Pierce. 1975. "The Illusion of Deterrence in Isaac Ehrlich's on Capital Punishment." *The Yale Law Journal* 85(2):187-208.

Bowers, William J. and Glenn L. Pierce. 1980. "Deterrence or Brutalization: What is the Effect of Executions?" *Crime & Delinquency*. 26(4):453-484.

Bright, Stephen B. 1994. "Counsel for the Poor: The Death Sentence Not for the Worst Crime But for the Worst Lawyer." *Yale Law Review* 103:1835-1848.

Bright, Stephen and Patrick. Keenan. 1995. "Judges and the Politics of Death: Deciding Between the Bill of Rights and the Next Election in Capital Cases." *Boston Law Review* 75:759-836.

Bureau of Justice Statistics. 2009 (Revised January 13, 2010). "Capital Punishment, 2008 – Statistical Tables." U.S. Department of Justice, Office of Justice Programs.

Census of Population and Housing, 1990: Summary Tape File 3 on CD-ROM [machine-readable data files] / prepared by the U.S. Bureau of the Census. Washington: The Bureau, 1992.

Census 2000 Summary File 3 – (United States) prepared by the U.S. Census Bureau, 2002.

Chambliss, William J. 1988. *Exploring Criminology*. New York: Macmillan.

Chavez, Alicia Fedelina and Florence Guido-DiBrito. 1999. "Racial and Ethnic Identity and Development." *New Directions for Adult and Continuing Education* 84:39-49.

Cloninger, Dale O. and Roberto Marchesini. 2001. "Execution and Deterrence: A Quasi-Controlled Group Experiment." *Applied Economics* 33:569-576.

Cloward RichardA. and Lloyd E. Ohlin. 1960. *Delinquency and Opportunity: A Theory of Delinquent Gangs*. New York: Free Press.

Cochran, John K., Mitchell B. Chamlin., and Mark Seth. 1994. "Deterrence or Brutalization? An Impact

Assessment of Oklahoma's Return to Capital Punishment." *Criminology* 32:107-134.

Cohen, Lawrence and Marcus Felson. 1979. "Social Change and Crime Rate Trends: A Routine Activities Approach." *American Sociological Review* 44:588-607.

Cohen, Lawrence and Kenneth C. Land. 1987. "Age Structure Crime: Symmetry vs. Asymmetry, and the Projection of Crime Rates through the 1990's." *American Sociological Review* 52:170-183.

Death Penalty Information Center. 2008. "Time on Death Row." Retrieved March 11, 2009 http://www.deathpenaltyinfo.org.

DeLamater, John. 1968. "On the Nature of Deviance." *Social Forces* 46:445-455.

Dezhbakhsh, Hashem, Paul H. Rubin, and Joanna M. Shepherd. 2003. "Does Capital Punishment Have a Deterrent Effect? New Evidence from Postmoratorium Panel Data." *American Law and Economics Review.* 5(2):344-376.

Dieter, Richard C. 2007. "Cost of the Death Penalty and Related Issues." Judiciary Committee; Colorado House of Representatives. House Bill 1094.

Dolan, Maura. 2010. "Lack of Funding Builds Death Row Logjam." *Los Angeles Times.*

Ehrlich, Isaac. 1975. "The Deterrent Effect of Capital Punishment: A Question of Life or Death." *American Economic Review* 65:397-417.

Ehrlich, Isaac. 1977. "Capital Punishment and Deterrence: Some Further Thoughts and Additional Evidence." *Journal of Political Economy* 85:741-88.

Fagan, Jeffrey. 2005. "Deterrence and the Death Penalty: A Critical Review of the Evidence." *Hearings on the Future of Capital Punishment in the State of New York.*

Fagan, Jeffrey. 2006. "Death and Deterrence Redux: Science, Law and Causal Reasoning on Capital Punishment." *The Ohio State Journal of Criminal Law* 4:255-320.

Federal Bureau of Investigation, Uniform Crime Report, 1950-2005. "Homicide Trends in the United States." Bureau of Justice Statistics.

Finckenauer, James O. 1988. "Public Support for the Death Penalty: Retribution as Just Deserts or Retribution as Revenge?" *Justice Quarterly* 5:81-100.

Gartner, Rosemary and Robert Nash Parker. 1990. "Cross-National Evidence on Homicide and the Age Structure of the Population." *Social Forces* 69(2):354-371.

Gastil, Raymond D. 1971. "Homicide and a Regional Culture of Violence." *American Sociological Review* 36:412-27

Geerken, Michael R. and Walter R. Gove. 1975. "Deterrence: Some Theoretical Considerations. *Law and Society* 9:497-513.

Gibbs, Jack. 1975. *Crime, Punishment and Deterrence.* New York: Elsevier.

Gotfredson and Hirschi. 1990. "The Nature of Criminality: Low Self-Control." In *A General Theory of Crime.* Stanford: Stanford University Press.

Gould, Jon B. 2008. "Justice Delayed or Justice Denied? A Contemporary Review of Capital Habeas Corpus." *The Justice System Journal* 29(3):273-286.

Grasmick Harold G. and George H. Bryjak. 1980. "The Deterrent Effect of Perceived Severity of Punishment." *Social Forces* 59:471-491.

Grogger, Jeffery. 1990. "The Deterrent Effect of Capital Punishment: An Analysis of Daily Homicide Counts." *Journal of American Statistics.*

Hackney, Sheldon. 1969. "Southern Violence." *American Historical Review* 39:906-25.

Hagan John and Celeste Albonetti. 1982. "Race, Class and the Perception of Criminal Injustice in America." *American Journal of Sociology* 88:329-355.

Halim and Stiles. 2001. "Differential Support for Police Use of Force, the Death Penalty, and Perceived Harshness of the Courts: Effects of Race, Gender, and Region." *Criminal Justice and Behavior* 28:3-23.

Haney, Craig. 2003. "Mental Health Issues in Long-term Solitary and "Supermax" Confinement." *Crime and Delinquency* 49:124-156.

Helms, Janet. E. 1993. *Black and White Racial Identity: Theory Research and Practice.* Westport, CT: Praeger.

Henderson, Martha L., Francis T. Cullen, Liqun Cao, Sandra Lee Browning, and Renee   Kopache. 1997. "The Impact of Race on Perception of Criminal Justice." *Journal of Criminal Justice* 25(2):447-462.

Hines, Crystal Nix. 2001. "Lack of Lawyers Blocking Appeals in Capital Cases." *Death Penalty Information Center*;   http://www.deathpenaltyinfo.org/node/541. Retrieved November 13, 2008.

Hirschi, Travis and M. Gottfredson. 1983. "Age and the Explanation of Crime." *American Journal of Sociology* 89:552-584.

Hollinger, Richard and John P. Clark. 1983. "Deterrence in the Workplace: Perceived Certainty, Perceived Severity, and Employee Theft." *Social Forces* 62(2):398-418.

Hraba, Joseph and Geoffrey Grant. 1970. "Black is Beautiful: A Re-examination of Racial Preference and Identification." *Journal of Personality and Social Psychology* 16:398-402.

Johns, Christina. 1992. *Power Ideology and the War on Drugs*. New York: Praeger.

Keckler, Charles N. W. 2006. "Life v. Death: Who Should Capital Punishment Marginally Deter?" *Journal of Law, Economics, and Policy* 2(1):101-161.

King, David. R. 1978. "The Brutalization Effect: Execution Publicity and the Incidence of Homicide in South Carolina." *Social Forces* 52:638-661.

Kornhauser, Ruth R. 1978. *Social Sources of Delinquency*. Chicago: University of Chicago Press.

Kozinski, Alex and Sean Gallagher. 1995. "Death: The Ultimate Run-on Sentence." *Case Western Reserve Law Review* 46:1-32.

Krivo, Lauren and Ruth D. Peterson. 2000. "The Structural Context of Homicide: Accounting for Racial Differences in Process." *American Sociological Review* 65(4):547-559.

Krohn, Marvin. 1976. "Inequality, Unemployment and Crime: A Cross-National Analysis." *Sociological Quarterly* 17:303-313.

Kubrin, Charis and Ronald Weitzer. 2003. "Retaliatory Homicide: Concentrated Disadvantage and Neighborhood Culture." *Social Problems* 50(2):157-180.

LaFree, Gary. 1999. "Declining Violent Crime Rates in the 1990's: Predicting Crime Booms and Busts." *Annual Review of Sociology* 25:145-168.

Land, Kenneth C., Patricia L. McCall, Lawrence E. Cohen. 1990. "Structural Covariates of Homicide Rates: Are there Any Invariances Across Time and Social Space?" *The American Journal of Sociology* 95(4):922-963.

Layson, Stephen K. 1985. "Homicide and Deterrence: A Reexamination of the United States Time-Series Evidence." *Southern Economic Journal* 14:68-89.

Lee, Matthew R., Timothy C. Hayes, and Shaun A. Thomas. 2008. "Regional Variation in the Effect of Structural Factors on Homicide in Rural Areas." *The Social Sciences Journal* 45:76-94.

Lee, Matthew R. 2000. "Concentrated Poverty, Race, and Homicide." *The Sociological Quarterly* 41(2):189-206.

Lee, Matthew and Ousey Graham. 2007. "Counterbalancing Disadvantage? Residential Integration and Urban Black Homicide." *Social Problems* 14(3):240-262.

Lempert, Richard. 1981. "Desert and Deterrence." *Michigan Law Review* 79:1175-225.

Lesane-Brown, Chase L., Tony N. Brown, Cleopatra H. Caldwell, and Robert M. Sellers. 2005. "The Comprehensive Race Socialization Inventory." *Journal of Black Studies* 36(2):163-190.

Levitt, Steven D. 2004. "Understanding Why Crime Fell in the 1990's: Four Factors that Explain the Decline and Six that Do Not." *Journal of Economic Perspectives* 18(1):163-190.

Liss, Marsha B. 1981. "Children's Television Selections: A Study of Indicators of Same- Race Preferences." *Journal of Cross-Cultural Psychology* 12(1):103-110.

Liss, Marsha, M.A. Newman, and F. Sherman. 1979. "Complexities of Children's Ethnic Awareness." Presented at the Western Psychological Association, San Diego.

Liu, Zhiqiang. 2004. "Capital Punishment and the Deterrence Hypothesis: Some New Insights and Empirical Evidence." *Eastern Economic Journal* 30(2):237-257.

Long, J. Scott. 1997. *Regression Models for Categorical and Limited Dependent Variables (Advance Quantitative Techniques in the Social Sciences).* Sage Publications.

Long, J. Scott, and Jeremy Freese. 2006. *Regression Models for Categorical Dependent Variables Using Stata, 2nd Edition.* Stata Press.

Loveman, Mara. 1999. "Is 'Race' Essential?" *American Sociological Review* 64:891-898.

Maltz, Michael D. and Harold E. Weiss. 2006. "Creating a UCR Utility: Final Report to the National Institute of Justice." Available at:
  http://www.ncjrs.gov/pdffiles1/nij/grants/215341.pdf.

Mann, Coramae R. 1993. *Unequal Justice: A Question of Color.* Bloomington: Indiana University Press.

Mann, Dave. 2010. "Solitary Men: Does Prolonged Isolation Drive death Row Prisoners Insane?" *Texas Observer.*

Marvell Thomas B. and Carlisle E. Moody. 1991. "Age Structure and Crime Rates: The Conflicting Evidence." *Journal of Quantitative Criminology* 7:237-273.

Massey, Douglas S. 1990. "American Apartheid: Segregation and the Making of the Underclass."

McCall, Patricia., Kenneth Land, and Lawrence Cohen. 1992. "Violent Crime Rates: Is there a general and continuing influence of the South?" *Social Science Research* 21:2816-310.

McCandless and Hoyt, 1961. "Sex, Ethnicity and Play Preference of Preschool Children." *Journal of Abnormal and Social Psychology* 62(1):682-685.

McNulty, Thomas L. 2001. "Assessing the Race-Violence Relationship at the Macro Level: The Assumption of Racial Invariance and the Problem of Restricted Distributions." *Criminology* 39(2):467-487.

Merton, Robert. 1938. "Social Structure and Anomie." *American Sociological Review* 3:672-682.

Merton, Robert. 1968. *Social Theory and Social Structure.* New York: Free Press.

Mocan, H. Naci and R. Kaj Gittings. 2003. "Getting Off Death row: Commuted Sentences and the Deterrent Effect of Capital Punishment." *Journal of Law and Economics* 46(2):453-478.

Morris, Aldon D. 1999. "A Retrospective on the Civil Rights Movement: Political and Intellectual Landmarks." *Annual Review of Sociology* 25:517-539.

Nagin, Daniel S. 1998. "Criminal Deterrence Research at the Outset of the Twenty-First Century," In *Crime and Justice: A Review of Research,* edited by Michael Tonry. Chicago: University of Chicago Press.

Newcomb, Theodore. 1961. *The Acquaintance Process.* New York: Holt, Rinehart, and Winston.

Osgood, D. Wayne. 2000. "Poisson-based Regression Analysis of Aggregate Crime Rates." *Journal of Quantitative Criminology* 16(1):21-43.

Parkin, Joan. 1999. "Clinton's Effective Death Penalty Faces Supreme Court Challenges." *The New Abolitionist* 13. Available at: http://www.nodeathpenalty.org/newab013/clintonAct.html.

Passell, Peter and John B. Taylor. 1977. "The Deterrent Effect of Capital Punishment: Another View." *The American Economic Review* 67(3):445-451.

Paternoster, Raymond and Leeann Iovanni. 1986. "The Deterrent Effect of Perceived Severity: A Reexamination." *Social Forces* 64(3):751-777.

Peterson, Ruth D. and William C. Bailey. 1988. "Murder and Capital Punishment in the Evolving context of the Post-Furman Era." *Social Forces* 66(3):774-807.

Peterson, Ruth D. and William C. Bailey. 1991. "Felony Murder and Capital Punishment: An Examination of the Deterrence Question." *Criminology* 29:367-395.

Peterson, Ruth D. and Lauren Krivo. 1999. "Racial Segregation, the Concentration of Disadvantage, and Black and White Homicide Victimization." *Sociological Forum* 14(3):465-493.

Phillips, David P. 1980. "The Deterrent Effect of Capital Punishment: New Evidence on an Old Controversy." *American Journal of Sociology* 86:139-148.

Phillips, Julie A. 2002. "White, black and Latino Homicide Rates. Why the Difference?" *Social Problems* 49(3):349-373.

Pitts, Robert E., D. Joel Whalen, Robert O'Keefe and Vernon Murray. 1989. "Black and White Responses to Culturally Targeted Television Commercials: Values Based Approach." *Psychology and Marketing* 6(4):311-328.

Radelet, Michael L. and Ronald Akers. 1996. "Deterrence and the Death Penalty: The Views of the Experts." *The Journal of Criminal Law and Criminology* 87(1):1-16.

Roberts, Julian. V., and Stalans, Loretta. J. 2000. *Public Opinion, Crime and Criminal Justice.* Boulder, CO: Westview Press.

Rosenfeld, Richard. 1986. "Urban Crime Rates: Effects of Inequality, Welfare Dependency, Region and Race." in *The Social Ecology of Crime*, edited by James M. Byrne and Robert J. Sampson, Pp. 116-130. New York: Springer-Verlag.

Russell-Brown, Katheryn. 1998. *The Color of Crime:Racial Hoaxes, White Fear, Black Protectionism, Police Harassment, and Other Macroaggressions.* New York University Press.

Sampson, Robert J. 1987. "Urban Black Violence: The Effect of Male Joblessness and Family Disruption." *American Journal of Sociology* 93:348-382

Sampson, Robert J. and W. Byron Groves. 1989 "Community Structure and Crime: Testing Social Disorganization Theory." *American Journal of Sociology* 94(4):774-802.

Sampson, Robert J. and William Julius Wilson. 1995. "Race, Crime, and Urban Inequality." In John Hagan, and Ruth D. Peterson (eds.), *Crime and Inequality*: 37-54. Stanford: Stanford University Press.

Schuessler, Karl F. 1952. "The Deterrent Influence of the Death Penalty." *Annuals of the American Academy of Political and Social Science* 284:54-62.

Sellin, Thornsten. 1959. *The Death Penalty.* Philadelphia: American Law Institute.

Sellin, Thornsten. 1967. *Capital Punishment.* New York: Harper and Row.

Shaw, Clifford R. and Henry D. McKay. 1942. *Juvenile Delinquency and Urban Areas.* Chicago: University of Chicago Press.

Shepherd, Joanna M. 2004. "Murders of Passion, Execution Delays, and the Deterrence of Capital Punishment." *Journal of Legal Studies* 2:283-321.

Shihadeh, Edward S. and Darrell J Steffensmeier. 1994. "Economic Inequality, Family Disruption, and Urban Black Violence: Cities as Units of Stratification and Social Control." *Social Forces* 73(2):729-751.

Sidanius, Jim, Michael Mitchell, Hillary Haley, and Carlos David Navarrete. 2006. "Support for Harsh Criminal Sanctions and Criminal Justice Beliefs: A Social Dominance Perspective." *Social Justice Research* 19(4):433-449.

Simpson, Miles E. 1985. "Violent Crime, Income Inequality, and Regional Culture: Another Look." *Sociological Focus* 18:199-208.

Smith, Amy. 2008. "The Anatomy of Death Row Syndrome and Volunteering for Execution." *The Boston University Public Interest Law Journal* 17:237-254.

Smith, A. Wade. 1981. "Tolerance of School Desegregation, 1954-77." *Social Forces* 59(4):1256-1274.

Sorenson, J. and R. Wrinkle. 1996. "No Hope for Parole: Disciplinary Infractions Among Death-sentenced and Life-without-parole Inmates." *Criminal Justice and Behavior* 23:542–548.

Stack, Steven. 1987. "Publicized Executions and Homicide, 1950-1980." *American Sociological Review* 52(4):532-540.

Stolzenberg, Lisa and Stewart J. D'Alessio. 2004. "Capital Punishment, Execution Publicity and Murder in Houston, TX." *Journal of Criminal Law and Criminology* 94(2):351-380.

Sunshine, Jason and Tom Tyler. 2003. "The Role of Procedural Justice and Legitimacy in Shaping Public

Support for Policing." *Law and Society Review* 37:513-548.

Sutherland, Edwin. 1925. "Murder and the Death Penalty." *Journal of the American Institute of Criminal Law and Criminology* 15(4):522-536.

Sunstein, Cass and Adrian Vermeule. 2005. "Is Capital Punishment Morally Required?" *Stanford Law Review* 58:706.

Tabak, Ronald J. 2008. "The Private Bar's Efforts to Secure Proper Representation for Those Facing Execution." *The Justice System Journal* 29(3):356-366.

Thernstrom, Abigail and Stephan Thernstrom. 2002. *Beyond the Color Line: New Perspectives on Race and Ethnicity*. Hoover Institute Press.

Thernstrom, Stephan. 2006. "Demographic Perspectives on Diversity, Racial Isolation and the Seattle Board's Plan to 'Cure' Residential Segregation: The Benefits of Racial and Ethnic Diversity in Elementary and Secondary Education." *US Commission on Civil Rights' Report*.

Thernstrom, Stephan. 2000. "New Life for the "One Drop Rule." *National Review*.

Thomson, Ernie. 1997. "Deterrence Versus Brutalization: The Case of Arizona." *Homicide Studies* 1(2):110-128.

"Time on Death Row." 2005. Retrieved May 18, 2009 from the Death Penalty Information Center Website at: http://www.deathpenaltyinfo.org/time-death-row.

Tittle, Charles, R. 1975. "Deterrence or Labeling?" *Social Forces* 53:399-410.

Tittle, Charles. 1980. *Sanctions and Social Deviance: The Question of Deterrenc*. New York: Praeger Publishers Incorporated, U.S.

Tonry, Michael. 1995. *"Malign Neglect: Race, Crime and Punishment in America."* New York and Oxford University Press.

Unnever, James and Francis T. Cullen. 2007. "Reassessing the Racial Divide in Support for Capital Punishment: The Continuing Significance of Race." *Journal of Research in Crime and Delinquency* 44:124-158.

United States Department of Commerce Economics and Statistics Administration: Bureau of the Census. 1997. *Statistical Abstract of the United States.*

United States Department of Commerce Economics and Statistics Administration: Bureau of the Census. 2006. *Statistical Abstract of the United States.*

United States Department of Justice. Bureau of Justice Statistics. *Capital Punishment in the United States, 1973-2004* (computer file). Ann Arbor, MI: Inter-university Consortium for Political and Social Research.

United States Department of Justice. Bureau of Justice Statistics. "Capital Punishment 2005," Appendix Table 4.

Waldo, Gordon. and Ted. Chiricos. 1972. "Perceived Penal Sanction and Self-Reported Criminality: A Neglected Approach to Deterrence Research." *Social Problems* 19:522-540.

Ward, Geoff K. "Race and the Justice Workforce: Toward a System Perspective" in *The Many Colors of Crimes* edited by Ruth D. Peterson, Lauren J. Krivo, and John Hagan. New York University Press: New York and London.

Weisberg, Robert. 2005. "The Death Penalty Meets Social Science: Deterrence and Jury Behavior Under New

Scrutiny." *Annual Review of Law and Social Science* 1:151-170.

Whittler, Tommy E. 1991. "The Effect of Actor's Race in Commercial Advertising:
Review and Extension." *Journal of Advertising* 20(1):54-60.

Whittler, Tommy E. and Joan Scattone Spira. 2002. "Model's Race: A Peripheral Cue in Advertising Messages?" *Journal of Consumer Psychology* 12(4):291-301.

Wilson, William J. 1987. *The Truly Disadvantaged: The Inner City, the Underclass and Public Policy.* Chicago: University of Chicago Press.

Wilson, William J. 1996. *When Work Disappears: The World of the New Urban Poor.* Chicago: University of Chicago Press.

Wise. David C. 2002. "Capital Punishment Proves to be Expensive." *New York Law Journal* 45:1-14.

Wise, David C. 2003. "Costly Price of Capital Punishment: Case Shows Efforts Expended Before the State Takes A Life." *Albany Times Union.*

Wolfgang, Marvin E. 1967. *The Subculture of Violence.* Newbury Park, CA: Sage.

Wolfgang, Marvin E. and Franco Ferracuti. 1967. *The Subculture of Violence: Towards an Integrated Theory in Criminology.* Beverly Hills: Sage.

Wortley, Scot., John Hagan, and Ross Macmillan. 1997. "Just Des(s)erts? The Racial Polarization of Perceptions of Criminal Injustice." *Law and Society Review* 30(4):637-676.

Yuzon, Florencio J. 1996. "Conditions and Circumstances of Living on Death Row – Violative of Individual Rights and Fundamental Freedoms? Divergent Trends of Judicial Review in Evaluating the 'Death Row Phenomena'." *The George Washington Journal of International Law and Economics* 39:57-69.

Zimring, Franklin and Gordon Hawkins. 1973. *Deterrence: The Legal Threat in Crime Control. Chicago: Chicago University.*

Index